WHAT TO DO WHEN JESUS IS HUNGRY

FATHER ANDREW APOSTOLI, C.F.R.

What To Do When
Jesus Is Hungry

~

A Practical Guide to the
Works of Mercy

IGNATIUS PRESS   SAN FRANCISCO

Cover photograph courtesy of
Project PEARLS

Cover design by Riz Boncan Marsella

© 2011 Ignatius Press, San Francisco
All rights reserved
ISBN 978-1-58617-449-1
Library of Congress Control Number 2010931421
Printed in the United States of America ∞

Dedication

In great filial devotion, I dedicate this book to the Sorrowful and Immaculate Heart of Mary, who exemplified the Works of Mercy throughout her life. Filled with compassion for her elderly cousin, Elizabeth, at the Visitation, concerned for the young married couple at Cana in their need, sharing the sorrow of her Son on the Way of the Cross and beneath it, and always praying for her sons and daughters as she did at Pentecost, our Lady is a living embodiment of these works of charity and mercy.

Contents

Acknowledgment

This author wishes gratefully to acknowledge the kindness of *Envoy* magazine and its editor, Mr. Patrick Madrid, because the content regarding the Works of Mercy contained in this book originally appeared as a series of articles in *Envoy* over a span of time from 1998 to 2010.

Introduction

Building the "Civilization of Love"
by the Works of Mercy

The new life in Christ we receive in our baptism is sustained by our practice of the three theological virtues: faith, hope, and love. They are called *theological*, from the Greek word *Theos* which means *God*, because they direct our Christian life in relation to God. By faith we believe God exists and that he cares for us. By hope we trust in his promises to save us by giving us eternal happiness in Heaven and all the graces we need to get there. Finally, by love or charity, we love God who is all-good and worthy of all our love, and we love our neighbor and ourselves (with a proper self-love) because we are made in the image and likeness of God.

In addition to the theological virtues, we must practice the moral virtues, of which there are four. Prudence directs us in making correct choices and decisions in life. Justice helps us deal with others in a proper manner, giving to each person what is his due. Temperance assists us by controlling our emotions and passions, which easily become disordered in pursuing pleasure. Finally, fortitude helps us overcome fears that keep us from loving God by instilling greater freedom and courage in our hearts. For all these virtues to operate properly, we need the inspirations and sanctifying gifts of the Holy Spirit. It is he who inspires and strengthens us to do good in a more consistent and joyful manner.

Ultimately, these virtues must find expression in what we call the *works of mercy*. What are these works of mercy? The Catechism of the Catholic Church offers this description: "The *works of mercy* are charitable actions by which we come to the aid of our neighbor in his spiritual and bodily necessities" (CCC 2447). Since the works of mercy must meet all our needs as human beings, we generally divide these works into two kinds: corporal and spiritual. The *corporal works of mercy* refer primarily to the needs of the body, while the *spiritual works of mercy* meet the needs of the soul.

Our Needs of Body and Soul

Our Lord himself enumerates six of the seven corporal works of mercy in his description of the Last Judgment.

> When the Son of man comes in his glory, and all the angels with him, then he will sit on his glorious throne. Before him will be gathered all the nations, and he will separate them one from another as a shepherd separates the sheep from the goats, and he will place the sheep at his right hand, but the goats at the left. Then the King will say to those at his right hand, "Come, O blessed of my Father, inherit the kingdom prepared for you from the foundation of the world; for I was hungry and you gave me food, I was thirsty and you gave me drink, I was a stranger and you welcomed me, I was naked and you clothed me, I was sick and you visited me, I was in prison and you came to me." (Mt 25:31–36)

Here Jesus speaks of meeting the true bodily needs of the hungry, the thirsty, the homeless, the naked, the sick and the imprisoned. The Church adds a seventh corporal work of mercy: to bury the dead. These needs, being essentially those of the body, must be satisfied in a material way. Interestingly, some of these corporal works of mercy also have a spiritual application, such as fulfilling the spiritual hunger for Holy Communion or the spiritual thirst for prayer. We will reflect on these spiritual applications of the corporal works of mercy in these chapters.

The seven spiritual works of mercy are given to us by the Church to help us live more fully the gospel command of charity toward our neighbor. They either meet needs that our neighbors may experience, such as for instruction in matters of the Faith, wise counsel, consolation in suffering, correction of their vices, and prayer for their various concerns and intentions. Or they help create conditions required to live in peace and Christian unity, such as patience to bear with one another's faults or the mercy to forgive others' sins.

The Works of Mercy Are Important

Many good Catholics do not realize how important the works of mercy are in the daily living of the Christian life. Let us begin, then, by looking at a number of reasons why the works of mercy help us to live the gospel more fully.

Love Demands Them

The works of mercy are important because they connect the love of neighbor with the love of God. In the Gospels, our Lord was asked the question, "What is the first of all the commandments?" (Mk 12:28; Mt 22:34–40; Lk 10:25–28) This was apparently a major theological question of the day, one which was hotly debated! The rabbis (teachers) and the scribes (religious lawyers) had gone through the Old Testament writings and various other legislative documents and come up with 613 precepts that had to be obeyed. The debate focused on which of these was the most important. The various scribes who put this question to Jesus were looking for only one answer. Our Lord, however, gave two commandments. Quoting one of them from the Book of Deuteronomy (6:5), he said: "You shall love the Lord your God, with all your heart, and with all your soul, and with all your mind. This is the great and first commandment" (Mt 22:37–38). That was the only answer the scribe was looking for, but our Lord went further. Quoting from Leviticus (19:18), he added: "And a second is like it, You shall love your neighbor as yourself. On these two commandments depend all the law and the prophets" (Mt 22:39–40). What our Lord is teaching us here is that we cannot separate the love of God from the love of our neighbor. One without the other is incomplete. They must go together, as we shall see elsewhere in the New Testament.

The Eucharist Calls Us to Charity

The second reason we must perform the works of mercy is because the Holy Eucharist, which is "the source and summit of the Christian life" as the Second Vatican Council described it, moves us from sacramental union with Christ in his Eucharistic Body to union with Christ in his Mystical Body, in the least of his brothers and sisters. This two-fold love, stemming from the Eucharist, is the fulfillment of the love of God and neighbor mentioned above. This two-fold Eucharistic love becomes the basis upon which to live our new life in Christ. It is not enough to have mere piety. To live fully in communion with Christ, we must reach out to our neighbor as well. We find this two-fold love expressed so beautifully in the First Letter of John: "God is love, and he who abides in love abides in God, and God abides in him" (4:16). To share in this love of God, meaning that God loves us and we love him in return, is the very reason we were created. This love is the source of all our joy and happiness, both in time and in eternity. Saint John continues: "If anyone says, 'I love God,' and hates his brother, he is a liar; for he who does not love his brother whom he has seen, cannot love God whom he has not seen. And this commandment we have from him, that he who loves God should love his brother also" (1 Jn 4:20-21). Once again we see that the love of God is completed in the love of our neighbor.

Sacraments, as defined in the *Baltimore Catechism*, are "outward signs instituted by Christ to give grace". The Church clearly teaches that we should receive Jesus in Holy Communion only when in the state of sanctifying grace, which means we have the Most Blessed Trinity spiritually living in us. Therefore, we receive an "increase" of sanctifying grace each time we receive Jesus in the Blessed Sacrament. The first effect of Holy Communion, then, is to deepen our personal union with Jesus. After all, through each reception of the Eucharist, we allow Jesus to live his life more fully in us if we respond properly to his love.

There is a second effect of Holy Communion, which is that the love for Jesus must be extended now to our spiritual brothers and sisters. Our Lord taught this in his allegory of the vine and the branches (cf. Jn 15:1ff.). Jesus said that he is the vine and we are the branches. Just as branches draw their life-giving sustenance from the vine, so we spiritually draw life from Christ in the Eucharist. But because all the branches are directly connected to the same vine, which is

Christ, then they are indirectly connected to each other. The life of Christ that is in one member of his Mystical Body is the same life of Christ that is in all the others. Therefore, the Eucharist compels us to love and serve one another as Christ taught us: "A new commandment I give you, that you love one another; even as I have loved you, that you also love one another" (Jn 13:34). He also said to the apostles after he washed their feet at the Last Supper: "If I, then, your Lord and Teacher, have washed your feet, you also ought to wash one another's feet. For I have given you an example, that you also should do as I have done to you" (Jn 13:14–15).

A beautiful illustration of this two-fold Eucharistic love, namely, for Christ and for our neighbor, is seen in the life of Mother Teresa of Calcutta. She was once asked, "From where do you find the strength to take care of all the difficult cases that you encounter each day? The dying destitutes in the streets of Calcutta? The lepers? The abandoned babies? The AIDS victims? The homeless and the hungry?" Mother answered with her simple yet profound wisdom, "I begin each day by going to Mass and receiving Jesus in Holy Communion, hidden under the simple form of bread. Then I go out into the streets and find the same Jesus hidden in the dying destitute people, in the lepers, in the abandoned babies, in the AIDS people, and in the homeless and the hungry. It is the same Jesus." So too for us, works of mercy must be the fruit of our Eucharistic love.

Mercy Received Must Become Mercy Given

Another reason we need to practice the works of mercy toward our needy brothers and sisters in Christ is because God himself deals mercifully with us. In one of the weekday prefaces used at Mass, we proclaim: "In love You [God] created us; in justice You condemned us; but in mercy You redeemed us, through Jesus Christ our Lord." What this means is that God created our first parents out of pure love to have them (and every other man and woman as well) share his eternal happiness with him. But when he put them to the test to see if they would accept his love, they sinned against him by pride and disobedience. Therefore, in his justice which is as infinite as his love, he had to condemn them, barring the gates of Heaven from them. Because of Original Sin, the consequences of which we all share, and because of our own personal sins, we all are under the same condemnation of God's justice. But God was moved by his divine compassion to redeem us by his infinite mercy. As Saint Francis was known to say, "Everything God gave us before the Fall, he gave us out of love; everything God gives us after the Fall, he gives us out of his mercy!"

Mercy adds two qualities to love. First, mercy often involves a need for forgiveness. For God to show us mercy after we sinned against him, he needed to forgive us our sins. When we, in turn, do a work of mercy for a needy brother or sister, there is often no sin on their part against us. But we must be ready to do these works of mercy for anyone who is in need, even someone who may have offended us. The unique love Jesus taught us to have for our neighbor includes reaching out to our enemies, to sinners, to strangers, and to the "poorest of the poor", as Mother Teresa of Calcutta called them.

The second quality mercy adds to love is compassion. Compassion comes from two Latin words meaning "to suffer with" or "to feel the pain or deprivation that our neighbor feels". In the Gospels, Jesus gives us many examples of compassion. He felt pity when he preached at great length to the crowds, who were like "sheep without a shepherd" (Mk 6:34). He multiplied the loaves and fishes because he was concerned that the crowd, who had been with him for so long a time and were now quite hungry, would faint along their way home (cf. Mk 8:3; Mt 15:32). Jesus was likewise compassionate in his mercy toward sinners, in his miracles for the sick and infirm, and in his raising of the dead to console their grieving family members and friends.

The Good Samaritan is one of the most beautiful images of Jesus' compassion (cf. Lk 10:30–37). Moved by our helplessness after sin, much like the helplessness of the man who had fallen prey to thieves who beat him, robbed him and left him to die, Jesus cared for us in our needs when he went to the Cross. Like the Samaritan in the Gospel parable who set aside concerns for his own time, convenience and even safety, Jesus reached out and provided for us in all our needs without counting the cost to himself. By our very baptism which unites us to Christ and gives us a share in his own life, we are called to imitate his compassionate love and service. This calling is especially critical in our time if the Church is to fulfill her mission as God's instrument of peace and unity in the world.

Pope Paul VI, at the end of Vatican II, said that the Council's deliberations and documents gave us the image of "the Church of the Good Samaritan". In other words, the Holy Spirit spoke to the Church, calling her to give greater service to the poor. The Council declared that the Church must have a "preferential option for the poor", thus fulfilling one of the desires of Pope John XXIII, who convoked the Council. Prior to opening the Council, Pope John XXIII made a pilgrimage to Assisi, where he placed the Council under Saint Francis' special patronage and prayed that he who was called "the father of the poor" in his own time would intercede for the Church so she would recognize herself once again as a Church "of the poor and for the poor".

Jesus Is Still Hungry and Thirsty

A fourth reason for the works of mercy is quite simply that Jesus is still in need in the neediest of his brothers and sisters. He tells us that he is still hungry, thirsty, naked, homeless, sick, and in prison in his disciples. He suffered these things in his own lifetime on earth and continues to suffer them through the members of his Mystical Body. We need to reach out to alleviate the needs Jesus is still experiencing by ministering to his least brothers and sisters. Not only do they depend on us to relieve their needs of hunger and thirst and the like, but we depend on them for opportunities to serve. Without such opportunities, our lives would be the poorer spiritually. Mother Teresa of Calcutta once told me: "We will only know in Heaven how much good has come to us through all those who are in need, such as the sick, the hungry, and the homeless. This is because we cannot do anything for God in Heaven! In Heaven God is perfectly happy! He has everything he wants! So what did God do? God became man! Now we can do something for him because he said, 'I was hungry and you fed me! I was thirsty and you gave me something to drink!'" What Mother Teresa was saying in her profound simplicity and wisdom was that we have as much need to give to Jesus in the poor as the poor have need to receive from us as Jesus' disciples! Mother Teresa frequently emphasized the sublime dignity we have of serving Jesus in the distressing disguise of the poorest of the poor through whom Jesus so often approaches us. As she once put it, "We should not serve the poor like they were Jesus. We should serve the poor because they are Jesus." The corporal and spiritual works of mercy are our ways to serve Jesus even now.

To Build a "Civilization of Love and Truth"

One of the themes that Pope John Paul II frequently emphasized is that we have a need to build what we call a "civilization of love and truth". When the Holy Spirit came at Pentecost, he created a community of love and truth among the very first disciples of Jesus gathered in Jerusalem on the occasion of that great feast. Despite their ethnic, cultural, and language differences the effect of his coming was to restore a unity of peace and charity that had suffered greatly because of Original Sin and personal sin. In these critical times, we are well aware of the danger of violence and terrorism and the whole culture of death, even the possible catastrophe of a nuclear war. Prayer, sacrifice, and reparation are essential to countering the negative effects of selfishness and sin in the world. But we must also reach out in a very concrete way to those who are in need. Practicing the works of mercy helps us to move out of a self-centeredness which emphasizes and focuses only on one's own personal needs and concerns, and directs us out toward the needs and concerns of others. It is through the daily living of these works of mercy and love that we will heal the ravages of war, of hatred, of violence, and ultimately of sinfulness. If we are to build a Kingdom of God, we must do the works of mercy the Lord has taught us. The result will be a world where peace and charity will reign.

Pope John Paul II would also emphasize that peace requires the recognition of the dignity of each person. The works of mercy provide us with the opportunity to let every person know that they are children of God and brothers and sisters in Christ. What will emerge from this will be a community of love and peace centered on Christ. As Saint Augustine said, "In the end, there will be only one Christ loving himself." This means that the love Jesus shares with us and makes real in our hearts will be shared with one another for all eternity.

THE CORPORAL WORKS OF MERCY

Give Food to the Hungry

Of all human sufferings, hunger and thirst rank among the greatest. They are also among the most widespread. Countless people in the world go to bed hungry each night. Many people also daily face a critical shortage of drinking water. It is no wonder that Jesus mentions these two human needs, these two tragic sufferings, first among all the ways we may serve him by attending the neediest of his brothers and sisters: "I was hungry and you gave me food, I was thirsty and you gave me drink . . . as you did it to one of the least of these my brethren, you did it to me" (Mt 25:35, 40). In this chapter, we shall focus on Jesus' hunger; in the following chapter, we shall consider his thirst.

Jesus Endured Hunger

Sacred Scripture tells us that Jesus was like us in all things except sin. He shared our human joys and pleasures as well as our sorrows and our pains, sin excepted. He wanted to experience all that we experience, including hunger. So he voluntarily "fasted forty days and forty nights, and afterward he was hungry" (Mt 4:2). He sanctified our experience of hunger by his own hunger.

Jesus was greatly concerned about those who suffered hunger. On more than one occasion he multiplied bread to feed the hungry crowds who had followed him for days while he was preaching: "Then Jesus called his disciples to him and said, 'I have compassion on the crowd, because they have been with me now three days, and have nothing to eat; and I am unwilling to send them away hungry, lest they faint on the way'" (Mt 15:32–38; cf. also Mk 6:32–44; Lk 9:10–17; Jn 6:1–13). On these occasions, Jesus worked great miracles by multiplying loaves of bread to feed the thousands who had followed him. Once a young boy offered Jesus all he had—five barley loaves and two fish—which did not seem very significant in the face of such a great need. In fact, Saint Andrew the apostle who had presented the boy to Jesus, remarked: "What are they among so many?" (Jn 6:9) The young boy generously gave all he had; Jesus responded by generously multiplying what he had given with such unselfish love.

In our own reaching out to those in need, we may feel we do not have sufficient resources. But if we start giving to the needy what we have, even when it costs us dearly, we often experience God's providence to replenish what we are giving away. In the Old Testament, the prophet Elijah asked a widow with an only son for a piece of bread to eat and a cup of water to drink. Due to a prolonged and severe drought, the woman had only a handful of flour and a tiny bit of oil left in her home. She was going to bake one last bread for her son and herself and then, without any more food, face the prospect of starvation. But the woman generously shared with Elijah what little she had left, and God rewarded her abundantly. The flour did not run out, and the oil did not run dry until the drought ended and the people could provide for themselves again (cf. 1 Kings 17:7–16).

The Early Christians Fed the Hungry

The first generation of Christians, no doubt moved by the example of the Lord, were very concerned to meet the physical needs of the poor. They expressed this concern in very practical ways. Saint Luke writes of the very earliest Christian community: "And all who believed were together and had all things in common; and they sold their possessions and goods and distributed them to all, as any had need" (Acts 2:44–45). As the community grew, new needs emerged, and so the poor widows received a "daily distribution" of food (Acts 6:1). So important was this service that when the apostles themselves could no longer personally provide it because of the growing demands on them for prayer and evangelization, the first deacons were selected to carry out this ministry (cf. Acts 6:2ff.).

The attitude of the early Church toward feeding the hungry and caring for the needy was summed up by Saint James in his challenging letter; it must be our attitude today as well. "What does it profit, my brethren, if a man says he has faith but has not works? Can his faith save him? If a brother or sister is poorly clothed and in lack of daily food, and one of you says to them, 'Go in peace, be warmed and filled' without giving them the things needed for the body, what does it profit? So faith by itself, if it has no works, is dead" (2:14–17).

The Hunger That Needs to Be Fed

Hunger can arise from different causes, including scarcity of food due to crop failures, drought or natural disasters.

Sometimes it is caused by man's failures such as deprivation or neglect. Deprivation occurs when those who have the resources do not share them with those who are less fortunate. In fact, sometimes the affluent use their resources to prevent the less fortunate from obtaining what they need. Lacking the necessary resources, these poor depend on the assistance and generosity of others, which may or may not be forthcoming. At other times, the suffering of hunger is caused by neglect, when people fail to provide in a responsible way for what they will need in the near future. Perhaps they do not take advantage of opportunities to acquire a modest income for themselves, or they spend their money excessively on the wrong things. They then find themselves in need. In such cases they, too, must depend on others to help them.

The hunger Jesus suffered during his life on earth differs significantly from the hunger of the poor. He freely chose his hunger, while many of his poor brothers and sisters do not. However, Jesus chose to suffer hunger in order to suffer with and for mankind. In his passion and death, he took upon himself all the sufferings of men, including the persecution of his disciples by Saul of Tarsus. Jesus said to him on the road to Damascus: "Saul, Saul, why do you persecute me?" Notice that Jesus did not say: "Saul, Saul, why do you persecute my disciples?" This is why the future Apostle of the Gentiles had to ask: "Who are you, Lord?" The voice answered, "I am Jesus, whom you are persecuting" (Acts 9:4–5). In a very real way, then, what we do to others, we do to Christ. When we feed the hungry, it is Jesus whom we satisfy.

Extreme Poverty Brings Extreme Hunger

I was in a very fitting place when I began to write this particular reflection: Mission San Serafin in Comayagua, Honduras.
The mission is staffed by priests and brothers of the Community of the Franciscan Friars of the Renewal, of which I am a
member, and I had gone down to give a retreat to the friars
there. Honduras is a developing nation, probably the poorest in the Western Hemisphere after Haiti and Nicaragua.
As you can imagine, many people in that country lack even
life's basic necessities, and many of the indigent poor in the
area come to the mission for help. Every month the friars
give five-pound bags of beans, rice, and corn; a two-pound
bag of sugar; and salt, oil, and laundry soap to more than
one hundred needy families. The friars have also brought
food supplies up to various mountain villages, where they
have been building homes and chapels, for the villagers are
in desperate need.

One case in particular illustrates the great need for food
that some Hondurans experience. One needy family the friars nicknamed "the meek family" because they are so humble and simple in their ways. The friars realized the children
were malnourished, but it was only after assisting the family
for two years that they found out the family would go for
two or three days at a time without proper food. As a result,
one of the young girls was losing her eyesight. When a medical team from the United States came to do volunteer work
in the area, an ophthalmologist examined the girl's eyes and
determined she did not have any eye defect, but that her
increasing blindness was due to malnutrition: She was lacking sufficient vitamin A. When the girl received increased

amounts of the vitamin, her eyesight came back. The friars are now regularly providing food for this particular family.

Feeding the Hungry in America

These examples are real life and death situations of hunger. The needs and the steps required to relieve those needs are quite obvious. But what about carrying out this same corporal work of mercy in the setting of wealthy developed nations such as the United States? The situation is so different. The question here is not one of life or death (Will I eat or not), but rather one of preference (What will I choose to eat?). When we go to the supermarket and see aisle after aisle of all kinds of food in every conceivable variety, we realize that most Americans are nowhere near the hunger level of people in developing countries such as Honduras. Does that mean, then, that we cannot feed Jesus in feeding someone who is hungry? In other words, are we deprived of carrying out this same corporal work of mercy in a developed country like the United States? Not at all, for even in a land of plenty there are people who are hungry. What can be done in practice to help them? Let us look at a few possibilities.

Helping at a Soup Kitchen

If there is a soup kitchen for the poor in your area, you might consider volunteering occasionally, or perhaps even on a regular basis. My community staffs the Padre Pio Shelter in the South Bronx, New York. We take in eighteen homeless men each night. We provide not only a bed to sleep in, but also a cooked supper, a simple breakfast and a brown bag lunch for each resident as he leaves in the morning. We have "food providers" that support our shelter ministry. These are individuals who either cook meals at home or buy the food needed for the meals. They usually drop the food at a location where someone can see that it gets to the shelter. Every night we also have volunteers who come in and help prepare the meals for the homeless men. Often as they leave after cooking supper, they will say how much they get out of being able to feed the hungry. In their own way, these volunteers feel they receive as much in return for feeding the hungry men in the shelter as the men receive in being fed. It can be a very rewarding experience. They know that they are feeding Jesus in his needy brothers.

Giving to a Food Pantry

Another way to feed the hungry is to give regularly to food collections, such as one for a parish food pantry that assists families or individuals who come upon hard times. This is especially helpful to those who live near the poverty line. Food supplements can make a big difference in their lives. If your parish does not have something like a food pantry, you might talk up the idea and start one, or even join with another parish that already operates a food give-away program. You never know how much good you can do until you try.

Shopping for the Elderly and Homebound

Feeding the hungry may also mean bringing elderly or shut-in people to a supermarket they could never get to on their own. In cases where such people cannot shop for themselves, a person might volunteer to do the shopping for them. If you do not personally know any elderly or shut-in people who might need assistance, perhaps you can check with the parish or local Saint Vincent de Paul Society to find genuinely needy cases in the area.

Voluntary Fasting

Still another way to reach out to the hungry is to deprive yourself occasionally, perhaps once a month, of some special meal or dessert. This can have a doubly good effect. For one, the hunger you voluntarily experience will create a sense of compassion and connection with those who suffer from a hunger over which they have no control. For another, any money saved by not having an expensive meal can be donated to people who reach out to the needy, like Mother Teresa's Missionaries of Charity. Your spiritual offering can then become a tangible way of sharing food with the hungry.

Make a Group Effort

One final possibility presents a significant challenge. Hunger will remain a constant need for many people. Only God himself can provide food for them all. But one important way to help at least some of them in a consistent manner is to stir up interest among a group of people, such as a parish community, to "adopt" a poor parish or mission in a developing country like Honduras. A number of parishes in the United States already do this. This is a serious and ongoing commitment, but it fulfills two needs at once: the need to receive on the part of those who do not have and the need to give on the part of those who have an abundance.

Christian Love Demands We Be
Aware of Others in Their Needs

Remember the parable of the rich man and Lazarus (Lk 16:19–31), in which Jesus describes two men in sharp contrast. The rich man was "clothed in purple and fine linen and . . . feasted sumptuously every day". Lazarus, meanwhile, was "full of sores" and "desired to be fed with what fell from the rich man's table". Eventually, when both died, Lazarus was brought to the joys of Paradise, while the rich man suffered the torments of Hell. Why was the rich man lost? Not because he dressed lavishly or ate well, but because he completely lacked compassion for someone suffering so obviously right in front of him.

Sharing generously with the hungry what God has shared with us is the wisest investment we can ever make. We will realize this when we hear those words of Jesus at the Last Judgment: "Come, O blessed of my Father, inherit the kingdom prepared for you from the foundation of the world; for I was hungry and you gave me food." And when the just ask our Lord when they did this for him, he will answer, "As you did it to one of the least of these my brethren, you did it to me" (Mt 25:34–35, 40). Pope John Paul II, in referring to these words of our Lord, said that they will mark the end of human history as we now know it. At that supreme moment, how blessed we will be for having fed Jesus in the hungry.

Blessed Are They Who Hunger for Holiness

Not all hunger is bad. There is a spiritual hunger that Jesus honors: "Blessed are those who hunger and thirst for righteousness, for they shall be satisfied" (Mt 5:6). This hunger, this longing for something good is not the physical agony of the starving. Rather, it can be compared to the hunger for a good meal, as in the Italian expression, *Buon appetito!* ("Hearty appetite!") In our spiritual lives, we need this hunger. Physical hunger which causes suffering must be satisfied so that the hunger will be removed. When it comes to spiritual hunger, we satisfy it not to take it away but to make it grow. As we look at various spiritual hungers that Jesus blesses, this point will become clear.

Hunger for the Word of God

After his forty days of fasting in the desert, our Lord was tempted by the devil to change stones into loaves of bread. However, he answered his tempter by saying there was far more important food than the bread that feeds the body: "Man shall not live by bread alone, but by every word that proceeds from the mouth of God" (Mt 4:4; cf. Deut 8:3). God's word becomes a nourishment that satisfies the hunger of the soul for truth so that we might know and fulfill the very purpose for which God has created us. Jesus himself said: "It is the spirit that gives life, the flesh is of no avail; the words that I have spoken to you are Spirit and life" (Jn 6:63). Saint Francis taught his friars that they should respect theologians who taught authentic Church teaching as those who minister to them "spirit and life".

Hungering for the word of God means desiring to hear that word. It is a longing and a welcoming of the word of God into our minds and hearts. Anyone who comes to love God's word has a certain relish for it. Hearing the word of God gives them comfort and consolation, courage and guidance. In this way the word of God becomes a source of light and love to do our Heavenly Father's will. In this sense we need that word to sustain us in our spirit. One who cherishes and lives God's word can echo the words of Jesus in his own life: "My food is to do the will of him who sent me" (Jn 4:34).

Being deprived of the word of God leaves us with a great hunger for it. We spiritually fulfill this work of mercy to feed the hungry by sharing the word of God with those who long to hear it. When priests preach their sermons, when catechists instruct the young in the faith or when sponsors help prepare converts for entrance into the Church, in each instance someone is ministering the word of God to others who are hungering to receive it. This hunger is not something we wish to eliminate. Rather, we satisfy it only to increase the intensity of desire. Like Saint Peter we come to realize that Jesus is the source of the Father's word coming to us: "You have the words of eternal life" (Jn 6:68).

For people who love God, being deprived of hearing the word of God would become a suffering like a great spiritual famine. The prophet Amos foretold that such a suffering would come upon the people of the Northern Kingdom of Israel because of their unfaithfulness to God: "'Behold, the days are coming,' says the Lord God, 'when I will send a famine on the land; not a famine of bread, nor a thirst for water, but of hearing the words of the Lord'" (Amos 8:11). Amos was prophesying that because of the people's

idolatry and immorality, there would not be anyone who
could preach or teach the truth of God's message to his people. Such a deprivation would be a terrible hunger of the
spirit.

Hunger for Jesus in the Eucharist

Even stronger than the hunger for God's word is the hunger
we experience for Jesus in the Holy Eucharist. Jesus said very
clearly in his teaching on the Eucharist that his Body and
Blood were true food and drink:

> "Truly, truly, I say to you, unless you eat the flesh of the
> Son of man and drink his blood, you have no life in you;
> he who eats my flesh and drinks my blood has eternal life,
> and I will raise him up at the last day. For my flesh is food
> indeed, and my blood is drink indeed. He who eats my flesh
> and drinks my blood abides in me, and I in him. As the living
> Father sent me, and I live because of the Father, so he who
> eats me will live because of me. This is the bread which
> came down from heaven, not such as the fathers ate and
> died; he who eats this bread will live for ever." (Jn 6:53–
> 58)

One of the greatest blessings the Lord has given to his
Church is to have his Body, Blood, Soul, and Divinity
present in the Holy Eucharist. The Lord gave us this beautiful gift so that we might share in two great mysteries, both of
which were foreshadowed in the Old Testament. First, the
Jewish people had the Passover meal in which they partook
of the Paschal lamb. The lamb was sacrificed as an offering to
God in atonement for sins. Then the people partook of the
flesh of the Paschal lamb to signify their share in that sacrifice. At the same time, the blood of the lamb was put around
the doorpost and lintels of their homes to protect them from

the angel of death who came upon Egypt and struck down the firstborn in those houses that were not marked by the blood of the lamb. Now in the New Testament, Jesus is the true Lamb of God (see Jn 1:29) who sacrifices his life on the Cross to atone for our sins. By receiving his Eucharistic Body, we partake in that redemptive sacrifice. Every time we receive Jesus in Holy Communion, we are cleansed more and more from our sins. A prayer by Archbishop Fulton J. Sheen to be offered after Holy Communion captures this truth: "May your Body, O Lord, which I have received and your Blood which I have drunk, cleave to my inmost heart and may no stain of sin remain in me whom this most pure and holy Sacrament has refreshed."

The second Old Testament prefiguring of the Eucharist was the manna in the desert. It was called "bread from Heaven", and the "bread of angels". But Jesus showed that it was only a shadow of the things to come when he said:

> "Truly, truly, I say to you, it was not Moses who gave you the bread from heaven; my Father gives you the true bread from heaven. . . . I am the living bread which came down from heaven; if any one eats of this bread, he will live for ever; and the bread which I shall give for the life of the world is my flesh." (Jn 6:32, 51)

Just as the manna in the Old Testament was the food for the people's journey through the desert to the Promised Land of Israel, so Jesus' Eucharistic Body is our food for the journey to the Kingdom of Heaven. If the Jewish people lacked the manna, they would have grown weak and would not have been able to continue their journey. In a similar way, if we lack the Eucharist, we would be deprived of the strength we need to sustain our spiritual journey. We could not resist the temptations of the world, the flesh, and the devil, nor could we practice the virtues of the Christian life unless we have the grace of the Eucharist to sustain us. It is a great blessing from God for a person to experience a real hunger of desire for Jesus, the Bread of Life. When we partake of ordinary food, that food becomes part of us for we are greater than the food we eat. When we receive Jesus' Body in the Eucharist, since he is greater than we are, we are transformed into his likeness. Through the Eucharist, we actually come to share in the very life of Jesus himself. There can be no greater hunger—and no greater satisfaction —than this.

We can spiritually fulfill the work of mercy of feeding the hungry by encouraging people to receive Jesus often in the Holy Eucharist. We should encourage people to be properly prepared to receive Jesus worthily, especially by being in the state of grace. We should encourage others, especially the young, to prepare themselves for receiving Holy Communion by consciously living a good Christian life. Finally we could also encourage a love for Jesus in the Eucharist by encouraging people to spend time in Eucharistic adoration. The bond with our Lord deepens when we are in his Eucharistic presence. Let us consider how many spiritual Communions we ourselves could also make before the Blessed Sacrament. In all of these ways we will be truly feeding the hungry in their need for the greatest food of all, the Holy Eucharist.

Give Drink to the Thirsty

If hunger is a great suffering, thirst can be even more so. I am sure we have all experienced an intense thirst on a very hot day! At the time, we felt real pain. Imagine people who experience this kind of pain on a daily basis. It is noteworthy that in the parable of the rich man and Lazarus, the only relief the rich man in Hell asked for was to quench his thirst: "In Hades, being in torment, [the rich man] lifted up his eyes, and saw Abraham far off and Lazarus in his bosom. And he called out, 'Father Abraham, have mercy upon me and send Lazarus to dip the end of his finger in water and cool my tongue, for I am in anguish in this flame'" (Lk 16:23–24).

God Provides Water for His People

Many times in Scripture the need for water became not only a challenge to the survival of God's people, but even a great trial of faith. We read, for example, that when the Israelite community left Egypt and was journeying through the desert, they encamped at a place called Rephidim. Here they experienced a great trial.

> There was no water for the people to drink. Therefore the people found fault with Moses, and said, "Give us water to drink." And Moses said to them, "Why do you find fault with me? Why do you put the LORD to the test?" But the people thirsted there for water, and the people murmured against Moses, and said, "Why did you bring us up out

of Egypt, to kill us and our children and our cattle with
thirst?" So Moses cried to the LORD, "What shall I do with
this people? They are almost ready to stone me." And the
LORD said to Moses, "Pass on before the people, taking with
you some of the elders of Israel; and take in your hand the
rod with which you struck the Nile, and go. Behold, I will
stand before you there on the rock at Horeb; and you shall
strike the rock, and water shall come out of it, that the people may drink." And Moses did so, in the sight of the elders
of Israel. And he called the name of the place Massah and
Meribah, because of the fault-finding of the sons of Israel,
and because they put the LORD to the test by saying, "Is the
LORD among us or not?" (Ex 17:1–7)

The Lord provided water miraculously for his people. He
was testing their faith in his providential care, but they failed
the test because they lacked the trust that God could provide
water even in such a desert spot.

Another incident of God providing water is found in the
Second Book of Kings. Elisha, the one who succeeded Elijah as prophet in Israel, experienced a trial with water at
the city of Jericho. Apparently the water was so bad that
the people could not drink it. Elisha took some salt and
threw it into the water saying, "Thus says the LORD, I have
made this water wholesome; henceforth neither death nor
miscarriage shall come from it" (2:21). And the Scriptures
tell us that the water from the spring remained pure from
then on. The Church makes reference to this purification
of the water in her blessing of holy water during one of the
optional penitential rites for Mass. (This rite can be used on
solemnities and at Sunday Masses.) The prayer that accom-
panies the mixing of some blessed salt into the water reads
as follows:

Almighty God,
we ask you to bless + this salt

as once you blessed the salt scattered over the water
by the prophet Elisha.
Wherever this salt and water are sprinkled,
drive away the power of evil,
and protect us always
by the presence of your Holy Spirit.
Grant this through Christ, our Lord.

Jesus Experienced Thirst

Twice in his Gospel, Saint John tells us that Jesus himself
was thirsty. The first time occurred when Jesus was passing
through Samaria and he came to a town named Shechem.
John describes the scene: "Jacob's well was there, and so
Jesus, wearied as he was with his journey, sat down beside
the well. It was about the sixth hour. There came a woman
of Samaria to draw water. Jesus said to her, 'Give me a
drink'" (4:6–7). No doubt, the long walk over dusty dirt
roads, under the sun around noontime in a country with a
very warm climate, created a great thirst in our Lord. His
request was for a refreshing drink of water. However, we
shall see that Jesus' thirst also had a spiritual sense.

The second time John mentions the thirst of Jesus is when
he was on the Cross. "Jesus, knowing that all was now finished, said (to fulfil the Scripture), 'I thirst'" (19:28). No
doubt our Lord was experiencing a severe physical thirst on
the Cross. He had not drunk anything since the Last Supper
the night before. Add to these long hours noonday heat and
the excessive loss of blood he experienced from his scourging, crowning and nailing to the Cross. His physical thirst
was undeniable. But as with his thirst at the well in Samaria,
Jesus' thirst on the Cross also had a spiritual aspect which
we shall see.

Satisfying Jesus' Physical Thirst

We can and must satisfy the physical thirst of Christ by satisfying the thirst that many of his least brothers and sisters experience, even on a daily basis. In many impoverished places in the world, water is a life and death issue. Let me share an example. A group of people, including some of the Franciscan Friars and Sisters of the Renewal, worked on a project to provide fresh drinking water to an extremely poor town in Haiti. Some individuals had heard stories of how many young children were dying of dehydration because they did not have clean drinking water in their area. So they formed a group of people who wanted to remedy the situation, and they were able to raise enough money to buy a water pump. Some members of the group even traveled to Haiti to help install the water pump and dig a much-needed well. They also took food and other supplies that the poor so desperately needed. Today, the children and their families have clean water to drink, and the death rate from dehydration has dropped considerably. No doubt, there are many similar situations where water for life can be made available when people work to find a solution.

Another similar situation exists near the friars' mission in Honduras. In the cities, the local governments often provide water pipes for the people; however, the people must pay the plumbing costs to have their homes connected to the city water pipes. Sadly, the poor often cannot afford to pay these costs. The friars in Honduras, with the support of benefactors, are assisting very poor families with the costs of connecting their water pipes.

How Do We Help the Thirsty in America?

These examples can inspire individuals and groups to become involved in helping poorer countries provide enough fresh drinking water for their citizens. Irrigation projects, especially in areas of drought, provide life-sustaining food and water. Many of the examples given in the previous chapter for providing food for the hungry can also be used to supply drink for the thirsty. Whether serving a glass of cold water to someone in a shelter, or making cool lemonade on a hot day for family and friends, or shopping for milk for a shut-in person, or offering a cup of coffee or tea to a visitor on a cold day, such a gesture can be done as an act of kindness to Jesus himself. And he assures us how special this simple act is and how it will not be forgotten: "And whoever gives to one of these little ones even a cup of cold water because he is a disciple, truly, I say to you, he shall not lose his reward" (Mt 10:42).

Voluntary Thirst

One special way to help the thirsty is to experience thirst voluntarily. This can be done as a simple form of mortification, such as not drinking an extra cup of coffee or skipping a refreshing glass of orange juice one morning, or even just delaying for an hour or so a glass of water. We can offer these little sacrifices in union with Jesus' own thirst to satisfy the spiritual and physical thirsts he still experiences in the least of his brothers and sisters. By doing this we can feel even in a very limited way a greater sense of compassion for those who suffer thirst out of sheer deprivation.

Perhaps more importantly, a person could decide to

deprive himself of an occasional alcoholic drink, or of a costly bottle of liquor or a six-pack of beer. (The amount saved would make a great donation to help the poor and needy!) Alcoholic drink has many ways of controlling a person's life. People who abuse alcohol to escape life's problems might find that depriving themselves can become an unselfish act of sacrifice that helps them to turn away from self-absorption or self-pity. Charity begins to blossom in a person's life when he can forget himself in loving others!

Support the Right of All to Food and Drink

The corporal work of mercy of giving drink to the thirsty finds new application today when we consider the plight of the sick and handicapped who completely depend upon others to provide their needs for food and water. As we know, those who are dying, those in a coma, those with severe handicaps or the like are at risk of being deprived of essential food and water. Anyone who is continuously deprived of food and water, no matter how good his health, will eventually die of starvation or dehydration. Yet the fundamental right to food and water is being denied in cases of extreme illness or disability.

The tragic case of Terri Schiavo revealed this disturbing trend. By court order, Terri's feeding tube was removed, condemning her to die from starvation and dehydration. And what a painful death! A friend of mine, a priest who was working with Terri's parents to preserve her life, shared part of his experience when he was in the room with Terri as she was dying in great suffering. He said that a policeman was stationed in the room around the clock to make sure no one tried to give Terri any food or drink. Near Terri's bed were vases of flowers with water in them. My friend said that if he had even tried to dip his finger into that water in order to refresh Terry's lips, he would have been arrested! What does this say about the direction we are going in with regard to the dignity of human life? Will not Jesus say of this situation, "I was thirsty and you allowed me to die of thirst"?

Terri Schiavo's case challenges us to do what we can to promote knowledge of the basic right to food and drink. At the same time, it should move us to be active in promoting a culture of life in our nation and throughout the world. Contacting politicians and judges, as well as working with church pro-life groups, can do a lot to promote this important work of mercy.

Satisfying the Lord's Spiritual Thirst

The work of mercy to give drink to the thirsty refers primarily to the physical thirst of so many in the world. But we can apply this particular work of mercy in a spiritual way. Let us first look at the thirst of Jesus.

Thirst for the Salvation of Souls

As we have already seen, the Gospel of John refers twice to Jesus' thirst. The first time is his thirst at the well in Samaria. While he was physically thirsty, there was also a spiritual dimension to his thirst, a thirst for the Samaritan woman's salvation. She was leading a sinful life, as Jesus pointed out: "You have had five husbands, and he whom you now have is not your husband" (Jn 4:18). Jesus was the Good Shepherd, and the Samaritan woman was one of his lost sheep. He had come precisely for the salvation of the whole world. His conversation with the woman led her to believe that he was the Messiah sent by God and it moved her to change her life. The water in the well that she had come to get that day no longer became important when he talked to her about another water, the "living water" of the Holy Spirit that she could drink and never thirst again. The living water of the Holy Spirit quenches our heart's deepest longing.

This same spiritual thirst of Christ occurred on the Cross. Again he was thirsting for the salvation of the whole world. Had he not said, "And I, when I am lifted up from the earth, will draw all men to myself" (Jn 12:32). Saint Augustine wrote that the whole appearance of Jesus on the Cross invites us to come to him: his head is bent down as if to kiss us, his arms are extended wide as if to embrace us, and his heart is pierced open as if to receive us.

The thirst of Christ on the cross became the central theme of the spirituality and apostolic activity of the Missionaries of Charity. To remind her community of the importance of the thirst of Christ, Mother Teresa directed that in all chapels of the Missionaries, next to the cross in the sanctuary would be the words of Jesus: "I thirst!" She taught her sisters that Jesus' thirst would be satisfied physically by giving drink to the least of his needy brothers and sisters. But Jesus' spiritual thirst would be satisfied by the love we give to him through our personal devotion and service to him, as well as our love and service to his least brothers and sisters. She also said the spiritual thirst of Christ would be satisfied through our working for the salvation of souls.

We ourselves must now continue to satisfy Jesus' thirst for the salvation of all men and women. He had said that he had come to give us life and give it abundantly (see Jn 10:10). We assist Jesus in the work of salvation by our prayers for the conversion of sinners, by our acts of virtue in doing God's will and by our sacrifices offered up to God in reparation for our sins as well as the sins of others. This is our co-redemptive mission with Christ. This was the heart of the message of our Lady of Fatima when she asked for prayer and penance for the conversion of sinners. She had told the children, "Many souls are lost from God because there is no one to pray and offer sacrifices for them." We can also satisfy Jesus' spiritual thirst by leading people to have faith in him, to enter the Catholic Church by instruction and baptism, or to renew their life in Christ through the sacrament of penance if they have drifted away through indifference or immorality. Through prayer and penance, we can do this as well. This will satisfy Jesus' thirst for the salvation of the world.

It is our mission to help satisfy the burning thirst of Christ for souls. Jesus is still experiencing his two-fold thirst even today in his least brothers and sisters. Jesus wants us to satisfy both of these thirsts for him through reaching out to the spiritually and physically poor and needy.

Satisfying the Spiritual Thirst of Jesus' Disciples

Just as we can satisfy Jesus' continuing physical thirst by giving drink to the least of his brothers and sisters, so we could also satisfy a spiritual thirst in their hearts as well. In the case of physical thirst, however, our goal is to eliminate that thirst by satisfying it with a drink of water. But with regard to spiritual thirst, our goal is to satisfy it in such a way that it may not go away but may increase. This spiritual thirst is a longing, not so much out of suffering but out of ardent desire. Let us look at two examples.

The Thirst for Prayer

Scripture, particularly in the Psalms, speaks of prayer as a thirsting for God. For example, Psalm 42:1–2: "As a deer longs for flowing streams, so my soul longs for you, O God. My soul thirsts for God, for the living God. When shall I come and behold the face of God?" Another beautiful expression of this is found in Psalm 63:1–2: "O God, you are my God, I seek you; my soul thirsts for you; my flesh faints for you, as in a dry weary land where no water is. So I have looked upon you in the sanctuary, beholding your power and glory. Because your merciful love is better than life, my lips will praise you."

Certainly one of the deepest yearnings of the human heart is the longing for God himself. As Saint Augustine said so well: "God, you have made our hearts for yourself, and they are ever restless until they rest in you!" Only God can give us this peace, and we must pray to receive it. There are many people who do not know how to pray, or even of the importance of prayer in their lives. They are actually seeking happiness from the depths of their heart, but because they do not know God, they are often looking in the wrong places for a happiness that eludes them. It is a great part of our mission in Christ to teach these people about prayer and how to pray. As they enter into the experience of prayer they will have an increasing desire to be closer to God. Prayer will be one of the greatest means to satisfy that desire here on earth.

Thirst for the Holy Spirit

Another spiritual thirst of desire or longing will arise in the hearts of Jesus' disciples. This thirst will be satisfied by the "living water" of the Holy Spirit whom Jesus gives to those who seek him, to those who come to him to be refreshed by the new life of sanctifying grace in baptism or by sacramental absolution in the confessional. As Jesus said to the Samaritan woman: "Every one who drinks of this water [in the well] will thirst again, but whoever drinks of the water that I shall give him [the Holy Spirit] will never thirst; the water that I shall give him will become in him a spring of water welling up to eternal life" (Jn 4:13-14). At the same moment that the spiritual thirst for God's life and love is quenched by the Holy Spirit entering the heart of the disciple, Jesus' own thirst for the salvation of the world is more satisfied!

The Mission Jesus Gave Us

We, as disciples of Jesus, are told by him to be "the light of the world" (Mt 5:14). By our actions, we point out to our secularized society the only path to real happiness, which is to follow God's law as seen in the teachings of Jesus. We are also called by Jesus "the salt of the earth" (Mt 5:13). As salt both preserves food and brings out its good taste, we by our works of mercy transform society, making it a place in which each person can experience his dignity as a child of God.

It is above all the need to satisfy the thirst of Jesus that will keep us on the right course. By following all that Jesus "did and said", we will build a "community of truth and love" as Pope John Paul II always challenged us to do. And the world will be better for it!

Clothe the Naked

In the prologue of his Gospel, Saint John makes two powerful statements. The first is the very first verse: "In the beginning was the Word, and the Word was with God, and the Word was God." In this one sentence Saint John teaches three great truths. (1) "In the beginning was the Word" means that the Word was from all eternity; the Word is eternal, having no beginning and no end. He always was. (2) "The Word was with God" tells us that the Word is God the Father's eternal Son, the Second Divine Person of the Blessed Trinity. As we say in the Nicene Creed, the Word is "God from God, Light from Light, true God from true God, begotten, not made, one in being with the Father." (3) "The Word was God" means that although the Word is a distinct Person, he is completely one with and co-equal to God the Father.

Thirteen verses later, Saint John makes his second powerful statement: "And the Word became flesh and dwelt among us" (1:14). The evangelist is saying that God became man. He took his flesh and blood from the Virgin Mary and now has a true human body like our own. In this way, Jesus Christ, the God-Man, gave to our human nature, and particularly to our human body, a great dignity. So momentous a happening was the Incarnation that Pope John Paul II called it the "greatest event in human history". Our body, then, in some way reflects the sacredness of the human body of Christ. It has a dignity that must always be respected.

We Clothe the Human Body to Show Respect

Clothing the naked is rooted, then, in the respect that we must show for the human body. There are four reasons why we must respect the body as good.

Created by God

First of all, God created the human body. In the Book of Genesis, we read the description of God's creation of mankind.

> Then God said, "Let us make man in our image, after our likeness. . . ." God created man in his own image, in the image of God he created him. . . . God saw everything that he had made, and behold, it was very good. (Gen 1:26–27, 31)

We know that the body suffered serious negative effects as a result of Original Sin. For example, when God created Adam and Eve, they could not suffer sickness or death. Now after the Fall we are subject to both. Furthermore, before the Fall, Adam and Eve felt no disordered passions. They were naked, and yet felt no shame or concupiscence in each others' presence. Now as a result of Original Sin, we experience disordered desires very strongly at times. Yet despite the fact that the body is now subject to sickness, suffering, disordered passions, and even death itself, it still remains good because God created it, and so we need to respect it.

Baptism Sanctifies the Body

A second reason we recognize the body as good is because by baptism we became members of the Mystical Body of Christ. All who are baptized are joined to Christ like the members of a body are joined to its head. This prompted Saint Paul to write:

> The body is not meant for immorality, but for the Lord, and the Lord for the body. . . . Do you not know that your bodies are members of Christ? (1 Cor 6:13, 15)

As long as we remain rooted in Christ by remaining in the state of grace, our bodies share in his holiness.

Temples of the Holy Spirit

Another reason the body is good is again because of baptism. Through this sacrament, the body becomes a temple of the Holy Spirit. Saint Paul describes this in very powerful words:

> Do you not know that your body is a temple of the Holy Spirit within you, which you have from God? You are not your own; you were bought with a price. So glorify God in your body. (1 Cor 6:19–20)

Wherever the Holy Spirit dwells, he sanctifies his dwelling place. It is the Spirit of God who makes us holy by filling us with his divine life and presence. Since the Holy Spirit dwells in our bodies as in a living temple, he makes our bodies holy and pleasing to the Most Holy Trinity. For this reason, we have great reverence and respect for the dignity of the body.

Destined for Heaven

A fourth reason the body is good and should be respected is because it is destined for eternal life in Heaven. As Christ raised himself from the tomb of death by his own resurrection, we believe he will raise us up also on the last day. Our bodies will come back to life again, but they will be transformed into a glorious state, sharing the very glory and dignity of Christ's risen body. Here is how Saint Paul describes what will happen to the body:

> What is sown is perishable, what is raised is imperishable. It is sown in dishonor, it is raised in glory. It is sown in weakness, it is raised in power. (1 Cor 15:42–44)

The body is destined for eternal life in Heaven. Since the body shares with the soul in the work of salvation, it will share in the glory of the soul in Heaven. Christ will raise our mortal bodies from death and make them like his own in glory!

It is out of respect for the body that we shelter it, as it were, with clothing. Clothing is a human necessity. And so to "clothe the naked" we shelter the body, and this is a work of mercy, a call of Christ. What are some ways to practice this work of mercy? We will look at three possibilities. First, we must provide the clothing people need to survive the elements of the weather. Second, we should help people to dress in an appropriate way. Third, we must do all we can to foster Christian standards of modesty in dress.

We Clothe the Body for Protection

The human body in many respects is very fragile. We are susceptible to extremes of cold and heat. We can suffer frostbite and hypothermia in winter and sunburn and dehydration in the summer. Therefore, we must guard our bodies against dangerous extremes. As a consequence, everyone needs to have adequate clothing. Saint Francis loved poverty as the virtue he saw present in Jesus' life. So, in his poverty he chose a simple religious habit for himself and his friars. But he also required that the superiors in his order provide clothing for the friars "according to places, seasons, and cold climates". As a result, in the course of time it became customary for the friars to wear mantles in winter.

The Example of Saint Martin of Tours

When we provide clothing for those in extreme need, we are providing for Christ in his needy brothers and sisters. During our present time on earth, we do not yet see Christ in his glory. Rather, as Mother Teresa of Calcutta would say, we see him in the distressing disguise of the poor. A great example of clothing the naked is seen in the life of Saint Martin of Tours (d. 397). The story is told that young Martin was drafted into the Roman army. Despite the fact that he was not yet formally a Christian, he tried to live more like a monk than a soldier. While stationed in the city of Amiens, he performed a great act of charity. One day during a bitter winter with severe frost, he encountered a poor man who was almost naked at the gate of the city. The man was trembling and shaking from the cold and begged alms from passersby. Martin, who was riding by with some other military officers, saw the poor man shivering in the cold. He dismounted from his horse and went up to the poor man. Then with his sword, he cut his fine military cloak into two pieces, giving one piece to the beggar and wrapping himself in the other. That night when Martin was asleep, Jesus, dressed in the half garment that Martin had given away, appeared to him and said, "Martin, yet a catechumen, has covered me with this garment." As a result of this vision, Martin made haste to be baptized. He went on to become a spiritual "soldier of Christ", a great bishop and saint.

Providing Needed Clothing

The most obvious way to clothe the naked is to donate clothing or the money to buy clothes either directly to those in need or to those who will distribute the clothing to the needy. If the clothes being given are used, they should nevertheless be clean and in good condition—not broken, torn, worn out, or blotched with unsightly stains. The clothing must always add to the person's self-respect. We can also try to donate the type of clothing most needed, according to the season.

Donating might mean joining in a clothing drive, or depositing something in a clothes drop-off bin, or bringing them to a distribution center. This could be done in conjunction with a Christmas party at a local shelter. Each resident in the shelter would then receive a supply of basic clothing. Some parishes have clothing rooms where they provide various items for the needy either free of charge or for a minimum price. You might even consider volunteering to help staff such a clothing center.

What are additional practical things we can do to clothe others with dignity? Many needs can be met related to a person's Catholic faith. For example, we can provide uniforms for Catholic school children whose families cannot afford them or a First Communion dress or jacket for a needy child. What about supplying Mass vestments for a priest in a poor mission area, or cassocks for altar servers in a poor parish?

Dressing Appropriately

We need to wear clothing not only to protect our bodies from the elements but also to express our dignity as human beings. Saint Paul mentions this when he writes: "Those parts of the body which we think less honorable we invest with greater honor, and our unpresentable parts are treated with greater modesty, which our more presentable parts do not require. But God has so composed the body, giving the greater honor to the inferior part, that there may be no discord in the body" (1 Cor 12:23–25).

The clothing that people wear can tell us something about their station in life. For example, we know two things that Jesus wore. At his birth he was wrapped in swaddling clothes (Lk 2:12). He was as humble and helpless as any newborn. We also know that Jesus wore a seamless garment when he was crucified. "When the soldiers had crucified Jesus they took his garments and made four parts, one for each soldier; also his tunic. But the tunic was without seam, woven from top to bottom" (Jn 19:23). In the time of Christ, the Jewish high priest always wore a seamless garment. Therefore, Jesus' seamless garment indicates that he, too, was a high priest offering himself on the altar of the Cross for our salvation.

A baseball player wears his uniform rather than jeans during a professional game. Members of the police force wear their uniforms so that they can be identified with their particular work. Traditionally, religious men and women have worn habits that mark them out as persons consecrated to God and belonging to a particular religious community. In all of these cases, clothes signify the work or identity of the person.

Example of Saint Francis

Clothing the naked serves not only the physical needs of the poor, but also their need for self-respect. An example in the life of Saint Francis illustrates this point. Saint Bonaventure, one of the biographers of Saint Francis, records an incident that occurred just before the conversion of the saint of Assisi while he was still a worldly man. God would call him through a great act of kindness to a nobleman.

> [God] afflicted [Francis'] body with a prolonged illness in order to prepare his soul for the anointing of the Holy Spirit. After his strength was restored, when he had dressed as usual in his fine clothes, he met a certain knight who was of noble birth, but poor and badly clothed. Moved to compassion for his poverty, Francis took off his own garments and clothed the man on the spot. At one and the same time, he fulfilled the two-fold duty of covering over the embarrassment of a noble knight and relieving the poverty of a poor man.[1]

Saint Francis not only helped to protect the man against the elements, but also recognized that this poor knight, being a member of the nobility, suffered embarrassment by not being dressed according to his proper state. Francis loved the

[1] Bonaventure of Bagnoregio, *The Life of Saint Francis* (*Legenda maior*), in *Bonaventure: The Soul's Journey into God, The Tree of Life, The Life of St. Francis*, trans. Ewert Cousins (New York: Paulist Press, 1978), p. 187.

fine clothing that he wore, but he willingly gave them to someone in need. As a result, Francis was rewarded with a prophetic vision from God for his life's mission. We have already seen in the example of Saint Martin of Tours that Jesus appeared to him holding the half of the mantle he had given to the poor freezing beggar. Francis received his vision as well. He had always wanted to be a knight and so God gave him a vision which he did not understand at this point in his life. Saint Bonaventure describes the vision:

> The following night, when he had fallen asleep, God in His goodness showed him a large and splendid palace full of military weapons emblazoned with the insignia of Christ's cross. Thus Christ vividly indicated that the compassion he had exhibited toward the poor knight for love of the supreme king would be repaid with an incomparable reward. And so when Francis asked to whom these belonged, he received an answer from Heaven that all these things were for him and his knights. . . .[2]

Saint Francis would later come to realize that he was not to head a literal army of soldiers with swords, but a spiritual army of friars who would fight the good fight of faith for the glory of God and the salvation of souls. God rewarded Francis' kindness toward the poor knight with a truly great grace. God also rewards our kindness with his graces.

Dressing Appropriately in Church

There is a special concern we should have with regard to dressing appropriately. In our present society many Catholics dress too casually for the Holy Sacrifice of the Mass. We must not lose the sensitivity that we are in the presence of almighty God. The very way we dress should show our

[2] Ibid., p. 187.

reverence and respect for him. It should also show our respect for our brothers and sisters in Christ who are sharing in the same Holy Sacrifice of the Mass. Therefore, shorts, T-shirts, or strapless dresses or blouses that do not properly cover the body should not be worn in church. Saint Padre Pio was not beyond asking people to leave the friary if they were not properly dressed. And he was not alone in this regard. When I visited the Orthodox monastery of Saint Mary Magdalene on the Mount of Olives, a monk was assigned to give a poncho to anyone he judged as not sufficiently covered to enter the grounds.

If improper dress has become a problem in one's parish, it would be good to ask the parish priest to say something from the pulpit or publish guidelines for proper dress in the bulletin. People would generally understand and agree with the importance of this message. Most of the time, all that is needed is for people to be made aware of appropriate conduct and they will respond accordingly.

We Clothe the Body for the Sake of Modesty

The Gift of Sexuality

Our human sexuality is a God-given gift. The gift of our sexuality is expressed in our bodies, in our maleness or femaleness. We read this clearly in the creation account in the Book of Genesis:

> So God created man in his own image, in the image of God
> he created him; male and female he created them. And God
> blessed them, and God said to them, "Be fruitful and multiply, fill the earth and subdue it." (1:27–28)

Pope John Paul II in his famous teaching known as the theology of the body says that even in its natural creation, the sexuality of the body in its masculinity or femininity reflects the very inner life of the Most Blessed Trinity. Therefore, the body has a dignity by the gift of sexuality that God has given us, reflecting something of his own inner divine life.

After the Fall, Clothes Are a Necessity

Before the Fall, our first parents were naked but felt no shame. Archbishop Sheen said that one reason they were not ashamed was because the glory of their souls, without any sin, shone through their bodies and became a kind of raiment or garment that covered them. It was only after they sinned that they both experienced disordered sexual passion, which made them feel shame in each other's presence. So clothing is now needed as a means of controlling lust, as are the virtues of modesty and chastity.

Our first parents did not feel shame in their original nakedness because their desires were completely under the control of their reason. They did not experience concupiscence, which is the disorder of our passions and our tendency toward sin. Let us look at three things that the Church teaches about concupiscence. (1) Concupiscence is not sin. Our desires for pleasures that contradict our reason, that go beyond what is good for us, are not in themselves sins. They set us up for temptations, but temptations are not sins either. (2) Concupiscence is the result of sin. As we mentioned, before the rebellion of our first parents there was harmony between soul and body. Adam and Eve desired only what was good for them. Sin, however, disrupted that harmony, and the passions were unleashed from the control of reason. (3) Concupiscence leads to sin. If we do not struggle for control over our desires, we will commit sins of lust, whether by thoughts in the mind, desires in the heart, or actions with our bodies. The concupiscence that Adam and Eve experienced after the Fall was transmitted to us, their descendants. We enter the world in a wounded condition, weakened by concupiscence. Modesty is a virtue that can help us and others resist the temptations caused by our disordered sexual desires.

The Virtue of Modesty

Modesty protects us and others from temptations to sins against chastity because it involves, above all, dressing in a way that properly covers our bodies. We must strive to maintain a sense of decency in our appearance as well as in our behavior. How we dress says a lot about ourselves and our intentions. When people dress immodestly, they draw attention to their bodies, making themselves an object of sexual desire for others. For example, wearing very tight clothes or very revealing styles that "unclothe" the body can easily stir up the sexual passions of other people. The immodestly dressed person, therefore, is in this sense an occasion of sin for others. We can see, then, that fostering modesty through proper norms of clothing for public decency is part of the practice of clothing the naked.

Current standards of decency, especially in the summer months, are terribly low even in public places. Little Jacinta Marto, the youngest of the three visionaries at Fatima, quoted many important statements from our Lady regarding modesty and chastity. The most sobering thing our Lady told Jacinta was that more souls were lost from God by sins of impurity than by any other sin. Our Lady also said that many immodest styles would come into fashion that would deeply offend her divine Son. Unfortunately, her prophecy has been fulfilled. Little Jacinta stressed that we must not follow the indecent fashions of the world if we are to serve God faithfully. She particularly warned women to observe modesty: "Woe to the woman wanting in modesty! . . . Women are worse than men on account of [immodest] fashions."

Modesty in the way we dress and even speak and act toward others protects us from falling into sin, as well as from being an occasion that could easily lead others to sin. We must not only practice this virtue, but also encourage modesty in others. This is especially important for those who work with youth—parents, teachers, counselors, clergy and religious.

Fostering Modesty in Youth

Here are some ways that we can foster the virtue of modesty in young people. (1) Parents should dress modestly both inside and outside the home and teach their children to do the same. (2) Parents should dress appropriately for Mass and require children to do so also. (3) Pastors should teach from the pulpit the standards of decorum that should be observed at Mass. If they are responsible for a school, they should make sure uniforms and dress codes are enforced. (4) Parents and guardians should monitor the shows, films and games their children watch on television and on the computer to ensure their decency. (5) Parents and religious leaders need to speak out against any forms of indecency in public. Whatever efforts one can make to foster modesty and decency in one's community will do much to promote respect for the body and human sexuality. Above all it will do much to help protect the innocence of youth.

Jesus Paid for the Sins of Sexual Immorality

We know that in redeeming us Jesus became a victim for our sins. He took our sins upon himself as the prophet Isaiah foretold:

> Surely he has borne our griefs
> and carried our sorrows,
> yet we esteemed him stricken,
> struck down by God, and afflicted.
> But he was wounded for our transgressions,
> he was bruised for our iniquities;
> upon him was the chastisement that made us whole,
> and with his stripes we are healed.
> All we like sheep have gone astray;
> we have turned every one to his own way;
> and the LORD has laid on him
> the iniquity of us all. (Is 53:4–6)

All of his sufferings redeemed us, but we might say that two in particular made atonement for sins against chastity. The first was the horrible scourging of Jesus, atoning for the sins of impurity, in which we misuse our bodies to seek unlawful sexual pleasures. The second was the stripping of his garments. These two examples demonstrate the terrible evil of sins against chastity by showing us the awful price paid for them by the Son of God. Saint Paul mentions "impurity" among the "works of the flesh" and adds, "I warn you, as I warned you before, that those who do such things shall not inherit the kingdom of God" (Gal 5:19–21). On the other hand, Saint Paul lists "self-control" (continence) as one of the "fruits of the Spirit". The Church adds modesty and chastity to the fruits of the Spirit. Practicing these virtues helps us not only grow closer to the Lord but also makes reparation for the many sins against purity. Perhaps we can end with a powerful thought from the great Curé of Ars, Saint John Vianney, who said that were it not for a few chaste souls, God would long ago have destroyed the world. Our struggle in this regard is for the glory of God and the salvation of souls.

Shelter the Homeless

Our Lord stressed our responsibility to meet the need for shelter among the least of his brothers and sisters when he told us: "I was a stranger and you welcomed me" (Mt 25:35). After our need for food and drink, the need for shelter would be the most important physical need we experience. We cannot live our life with dignity and security in this world without some place that provides us protection from the elements as well as a place we can call "our own", even if temporarily. After all, Saint Peter reminds us we are only pilgrims and strangers in this world. We have no permanent place here. Our permanent home is in Heaven. But in the meantime we need adequate shelter.

Jesus Was Homeless

It is said that the world gives everyone two things: a place to be born and a place to die. In a sense our Lord was deprived of both of these things. The Scriptures tell us that when he was born in Bethlehem, there was no place for him in the inn where travelers would gather (see Lk 2:7). Instead, he was born in a stable where the animals were sheltered. At his death, he again had no place of his own to be buried. The Scriptures tell us that he was buried in a tomb belonging to someone else. "Now in the place where he was crucified, there was a garden, and in the garden a new tomb where no one had ever been laid. So because of the Jewish day of Preparation, as the tomb was close at hand, they laid Jesus there" (Jn 19:41–42)

Even during his childhood, Jesus experienced a form of homelessness. When King Herod was infuriated at the news of the birth of a new king in Israel, he sent soldiers to Bethlehem to kill all the boys in that area two years old and younger (see Mt 2:16–18). As a result, the Lord sent his angel to Saint Joseph in a dream telling him to take the Christ Child and his mother and to flee into Egypt for safety. They remained there until the death of Herod, which occurred, according to some estimates, two years later. During this time the Holy Family were refugees. They no doubt experienced the difficult struggles known by refugees all over the world.

During his public life, Jesus was again homeless: "Foxes have holes, and birds of the air have nests; but the Son of man has nowhere to lay his head" (Mt 8:20). Our Lord probably slept out in the fields under trees, wrapped in his mantle for protection, as was the custom of the poor in his day. So when we receive the poor and give them lodging, we can say in the words of Saint Benedict, "Let every stranger be received as Christ!"

Outstanding Examples of Sheltering the Homeless

The Catholic Church has always had members who sought to provide adequate shelter for the homeless. For example, Saint Joseph Cottolengo (d. 1842) built an entire walled-in city within the city of Turin, Italy, called the Little Houses of Divine Providence, to care for orphans, the physically ill, and even the severely deformed from throughout Italy.

These "little houses" exist today, run by trust in God's providential care. A priest friend of mine who visited there mentioned how trucks loaded with food would begin lining up around four o'clock in the morning, and sometimes workers in those "little houses" did not know where these trucks were coming from!

Another example is that of Saint Padre Pio, who, seeing many sick and suffering people in his surrounding area of southern Italy, expressly asked his religious superiors to build a large medical facility for the very poor. He did not call the medical facility a hospital, but rather a "House for the Relief of Suffering" so as to stress that he wanted to assist the people in all their needs—physically, emotionally, and spiritually—as if they were in their own homes!

Possibly the most famous examples of homes for the needy are those founded by Mother Teresa of Calcutta. I had the opportunity to go to Calcutta and visit many of her homes for the different needy groups. Most remarkable of all was the home she founded for those "poorest of the poor", who were literally destitute men and women dying in the streets of Calcutta. The civil authorities gave Mother Teresa the use of an abandoned temple dedicated to Kali, the Hindu goddess of death. Mother Teresa changed the name to Nirmal Hriday (Pure Heart) Home for the Dying. She would often tell the story of a man who was taken into the home quite close to the time of his death. He only lived for two hours being cared for by the Missionaries of Charity, but he said to Mother Teresa, "I have lived all my life like an animal in the streets, but I die like an angel!" I remember seeing in this home where the "poorest of the poor" receive care, comfort and dignity, a sign which read, "Mother Teresa's First Love!" Mother Teresa's Sisters, the Missionaries of Charity, also provide housing or shelter for abandoned children, lepers, AIDS patients as well as for the general homeless population.

Recognizing the Problem

The homeless are very real, and it is a terribly distressing sight to see men and, even more so, "bag ladies" sleeping in city doorways or niches of buildings, wrapped in blankets on cold concrete, especially in winter. As we have seen, it is important to provide the basic essential protection from the elements, like extreme cold and heat, snow and rain. But it is also necessary to provide a sense of safety and security, a dwelling place of love, care and respect for the dignity of each person. This is why the first rule for the residents of the Padre Pio Shelter is: "Peace and respect will reign in this shelter!"

How Can We Shelter the Homeless Today?

The first step toward sheltering the homeless is to recognize the problem in your area. Next, learn whether or not there is a shelter near to where you live. If there is, you may want to call or pay a visit to see what you can do to help. Perhaps you may be moved to volunteer some of your time and service. There is always a need for volunteers to help in cooking meals (which can include making brown-bag lunches for the next day), or getting clothes for the residents (if there is a clothing room associated with the shelter).

Meeting the Other Needs of the Homeless

The first things the homeless need are four walls and a roof over their heads. These provide protection from the bitter cold of winter with snow and ice as well as wind and rain, and from the excessive heat of summer. But their needs do not stop there. Though some may choose to remain aloof and to themselves while in a shelter, many look for a place where they are accepted. This is because they suffer from what Mother Teresa called one of the worst forms of poverty, namely, loneliness. God himself had said it is not good for man to be alone (see Gen 2:18). People can sense when genuine caring and true hospitality are being extended to them. No matter where they come from or whatever their background, the shelter is "home" for them while they are there. This is why in fulfilling this work of mercy we must reach out with a welcoming attitude.

Many residents appreciate when someone is there to listen to their needs and concerns, or just discuss some of the issues of the day; so shelters need volunteers who can talk with the residents. There may also be the opportunity to pray with the residents. At the Padre Pio Shelter that my community staffs in the South Bronx, New York, we invite the residents and the volunteers to join the friars on duty in reciting Night Prayer in our little shelter chapel. There is usually a good response from residents and volunteers alike.

There may be bitterness on the part of many homeless, or frustration with their situation. This can be softened or even broken down by kindness. Mother Teresa, when asked why she did not join with civil government programs to meet the needs of the poor and homeless, answered that she and her Sisters had something to give the government does not: Christlike love and care. A piece of bread to eat and a bed to sleep in are only a beginning of a response to the needs of the homeless. More deeply, they also need to experience a sense of their own dignity as children of God, despite their material situation. This requires that we reach out to them with the attitude of Christ, who did not disdain to eat and drink even with people who were considered outcasts in society.

A Self-Giving Love Is Needed

To offer companionship to the homeless demands a love beyond the ordinary. It demands a self-sacrificing love. It is the kind of love Jesus describes in the Sermon on the Mount when he says: "But I say to you, Love your enemies and pray for those who persecute you, so that you may be sons of your Father who is in Heaven; for he makes his sun rise on the evil and on the good, and sends rain on the just and on the unjust. For if you love those who love you, what reward have you? Do not even the tax collectors do the same? And if you salute only your brethren, what more are you doing than others? Do not even the Gentiles do the same? You, therefore must be perfect, as your heavenly Father is perfect" (Mt 5:44-48). This can be better understood when we recall two Greek words used for the word "love" in the New Testament. One Greek word is *philia*, which is ordinarily translated as "friendship". This is a love that is shared with those whom we know, love and care for. It includes a giving and receiving. A perfect example is when Jesus tells the apostles at the Last Supper, "No longer do I call you servants, for the servant does not know what his master is doing; but I have called you friends, for all that I have heard from my Father I have made known to you" (Jn 15:15). The other Greek word is *agape*, which is self-giving, self-sacrificing love. This is a love shown for people we do not necessarily know, or with whom we do not enjoy a mutual love. It is shown to strangers and to those who cannot make a return of favor to us, such as the poor. It even goes out to sinners and those who have hurt us. This is a uniquely

Christian expression of love. This is often heroic. Jesus had this kind of love for us when he died on the cross for our salvation!

To help the poor experience a sense of their dignity and self-worth will require some degree of agape love. Those who work with the homeless may have to overcome some initial resistance from those they are trying to help, and they may need to gently break down barriers of hostility or resentment. This means being patient with people's faults, thoughtlessness, ingratitude, or rudeness. If you work long enough in a shelter, you will experience all of these responses. Some of the homeless may even be angry at you, despite all the help and kindness you show them, because they resent their situation and take it out on those who reach out to them. It is no wonder that Saint Vincent de Paul, the "Apostle of Charity" who lived with many abject poor would say, "We must ask the poor to forgive us for the kindness we show them."

All this requires courage, generosity, and an unselfish spirit. This is what is called a "disinterested love", which is a love that never asks, "What's in it for me?" It is a love that gives and does not count the cost!

From all that has been said, it is clear that not everyone can do the actual hands-on work in a shelter. A person has to be a little "tough-skinned" to work with the homeless. If a person is too afraid, working with strangers can be intimidating. If someone is very sensitive, he can be easily offended by a lack of manners, or a lack of gratitude, or simply by a bad attitude on the part of some of the homeless. Perhaps these persons would do better working in an auxiliary role, such as cleaning the shelter, stocking food, preparing clothing for the homeless or helping out in other ways behind the scenes.

If someone cannot actually do the hands-on work in a shelter, perhaps he can be a provider of food, clothing, sheets and towels, and the many other essentials that are always needed. Maybe they can organize a collection drive to gather whatever the shelter needs, or work with others to find permanent benefactors to provide for the shelter.

Those who are more comfortable interacting with shelter residents can find creative ways to assist. If people have a talent (such as art or music), they might volunteer their time and gifts to enrich the lives of those who usually have very little with a performance or lesson. Even playing a game of chess or checkers can be a meaningful contribution. In shelters for unwed mothers, assisting with the children can be a very rewarding experience.

You Can Receive More than You Give

The Missionaries of Charity told the story of a woman from the United States who went to Calcutta to work with orphan children at a home set up by Mother Teresa. The woman herself suffered from a rather severe depression. She worked almost exclusively with one child who was autistic. Eventually, after a long period of intense effort, the woman succeeded in getting the child to begin to communicate. A couple of years later, the woman returned to the United States. She herself was greatly changed—she had found a purpose for her life. She missed the child so much that she went back to Calcutta and, although Mother Teresa usually did not do so, she allowed the woman to adopt the child and bring that child back to the United States. One never knows what effect working with the poor and needy can do for our own lives.

Much more can be said about other ways of sheltering

the homeless, such as working to see that there is sufficient low-cost housing for the poor in your area, or working with groups like Catholic Relief Services or the Saint Vincent de Paul Society to provide immediate housing in times of fire, floods and other disasters. The basis, however, for all of this is remembering we provide whatever we do as our outreach to Jesus himself: "I was homeless and you took me in!" In this way, you are personally involved in building "the civilization of love" that Pope John Paul II has directed all members of the Church to do.

Opening the Doors of Our Home

Working in a shelter may be a special way of working with the homeless, but it is by no means the only way. The question comes up: Should people open the doors of their homes to the homeless? In answer to this question we would have to say that as a general principle, we should not open our doors to receive total strangers. This would certainly be against the virtue of prudence. In our society today there are many troubled people. If the person is a stranger, we would not know if he would do physical or moral harm to us or some other member of our family. They might rob or destroy property that is not their own. Our personal physical and moral safety would tell us we need to be extremely careful before we receive someone into our home. On the other hand, we might receive someone in special circumstances. For example, an exchange student who comes to us with a recommendation from an agency or people who know the individual would be safe to receive. In the case of a total stranger, we could still help by trying to find assistance at local shelters and other social services.

The Lord wants us to be ready to receive him. We have

seen there are many ways we can do so, while being prudent and safeguarding the well-being of all individuals involved. Whatever we can do to help those without a home, the Lord assures us that he will take it as being offered to himself.

Visit the Sick

One of the most difficult of all human experiences is loneliness. No one wants to feel left alone, abandoned, unloved. When only Adam existed, God said, "It is not good that the man should be alone; I will make him a helper fit for him" (Gen 2:18). We can say, then, that by our very nature, we experience a need to be with others, to interact with them, to accept them and be accepted by them. This desire affords us some very important ingredients for living our lives fully, namely, affection and affirmation. The care, concern and love we receive from others makes us realize that we are somebody, that we count, that our presence is an important gift to be shared with others. Persons who minister this affective, affirming love to us are like friends who double our joys and divide our sorrows!

The ill effects of loneliness are intensified when joined to further sufferings like sickness, infirmity or advanced age. To help someone deal with these painful experiences, then, is a great work of mercy. Those who offer their loving presence, care and concern to the sick will certainly merit to hear the words of Jesus at the Last Judgment: "I was sick and you visited me" (Mt 25:36).

Union with Christ

Jesus is often referred to as "the Man of Sorrows". Sorrow and suffering were unknown to our first parents before the Fall, but as a result of Original Sin, they are part of the human condition and are used by God to purify us from our sinful attachments and draw us out of our self-centeredness. In his great love for us, and in order to restore us to the fullness of life, Jesus shared the misery we had brought upon ourselves. He whom Saint John the Baptist called the "Lamb of God" (Jn 1:29) offered himself as a victim to his Heavenly Father to atone for our sins. Our Blessed Lord now asks us to share in his redemptive Passion and death in various ways. Among the most important of these are sickness, infirmity and old age.

We know that suffering in itself is not a good, but an evil. Thus Jesus would heal the sick and restore them to wholeness. He gave them "shalom" or that integral peace—physical, emotional, and spiritual—which our first parents enjoyed before the Fall. However, in the light of Jesus' sufferings, those of the members of his Mystical Body, when joined to his own, have a precious redemptive value. Saint Paul expresses this when he writes, "Now I rejoice in my sufferings for your sake, and in my flesh I complete what is lacking in Christ's afflictions for the sake of his body, that is, the Church" (Col 1:24). Paul describes "co-redemptive suffering", and it is very important in God's plan for the salvation and sanctification of the world. Just as Jesus used the five loaves of bread and two fish given him by a young boy and fed five thousand people (see Jn 6:8–9), so the Lord accepts our daily sufferings and sacrifices, no matter how insignificant they may appear to be, and joins them to his own for the world's redemption. This is why Saint Padre Pio, no stranger to illness and other great sufferings, used to say, "Jesus wants my sufferings! Jesus needs my sufferings!"

In the Sick We Encounter the Suffering Jesus

We may truly, then, look upon our brothers and sisters who bear the cross of sickness, infirmity or advanced age, as sharing Jesus' Cross in a more intimate way. By visiting them, we are visiting Jesus himself in his sufferings. What we do for them, we do for Jesus himself. Let us take a couple of examples from the devotion of the Stations of the Cross. Did you ever reflect on the Fifth Station, "Simon of Cyrene Helps Jesus to Carry the Cross", and say to yourself, "If only I could have been there to help Jesus carry the Cross which he carried for me"? When you go to visit the sick in a hospital, in their home or in a nursing facility, and you try to cheer them up by helping them get their minds off their difficulties or giving them a few words of encouragement, you are helping Jesus carry the Cross in his suffering brother or sister. Or have you ever meditated on the Sixth Station, "Veronica Wipes the Face of Jesus", and said to yourself, "If only I could have offered that service of love to Jesus"? You can do precisely that when you bring articles needed by the infirm and homebound, or even do their shopping for them. If they are in their home, perhaps you can help them with some housework or laundry. When I was young, my mother suffered a broken leg, and a group of neighbors came by to help with household tasks my mother could not do. It was both a great help and, to me, a great example.

Obstacles to Visiting the Sick

Human Suffering Can Be Difficult to Accept

Some people are afraid to visit the sick or infirm because they find it hard to accept human suffering. No doubt, it can be painful to deal with suffering, especially when it afflicts persons we love. But sickness in its many manifestations is a fact of life. The suffering person has not lost his dignity as a child of God. In fact, as already mentioned, these persons are actually being blessed to share the Cross more personally with Jesus! The late Archbishop of New York, Terence Cardinal Cooke, now a Servant of God in the process of canonization, suffered from cancer for a number of years. His experience led him to say shortly before he died on October 6, 1985: "Life is no less beautiful when it is accompanied by illness or weakness, hunger or poverty, physical or mental diseases, loneliness or old age."

Feeling Helpless to Help the Sick

Other people may not visit the sick because they feel uncomfortable in the presence of illness or infirmity they cannot remedy. They experience a feeling of helplessness, that nothing they do can make the suffering person get better. It is important to remember that we are not expected to cure the sick when we visit them. But to stay away from them at a time they need us most is to deprive them of blessings we can bring, blessings that are actually very helpful to alleviate their feelings of fear and loneliness. We can bring them the comfort of our company just by being at their bedside. We also may be able to bring the solace of our words and the encouragement to trust God through it all. Obviously, we will want to be careful not to burden them with our own problems, but direct our conversation toward lightening their load.

An Opportunity for Grace to Work

A time of sickness and suffering is often a time for extraordinary graces and even great conversions. Saint Ignatius of Loyola, for example, experienced the beginning of his great conversion when he was convalescing from a serious leg wound sustained in military battle. He liked to read books of romance and adventure, but a devout relative removed all such books from his surroundings, and left him with only two books: one on the life of Christ and the other on the lives of the saints. At first, because of his worldly attitude, he read these books reluctantly just to pass the time, as he had no taste for the spiritual life. Gradually, however, he began to feel the attraction of our Lord and the inspiration of the saints. Finally, he arrived at that point when he asked himself: "If the saints could do it, why can't I do it?" His conversion was at hand.

Praying with the Sick

Because prayer can open the soul to grace, when visiting the sick, always ask if you can pray with them. If they refuse, then ask if you can pray for them. If they even refuse that, then say a prayer quietly to yourself at their bedside. You can bring good literature for them to read, or even tapes to listen to while they are confined by illness or infirmity. How much precious time is wasted looking at trivial and often spiritually unsettling things on television. Instead, sickness can be an opportunity to lean more about God. Saint Bonaventure was known to say that adversity (sickness) prepares a person to receive the Holy Spirit.

Perhaps our visits can help persons who are critically ill and near the end of life's journey to make their peace with God by a good confession, especially if they have not received that sacrament of God's mercy for some time. Alerting a priest, either connected with the hospital or nursing home, or simply from the local parish, can help to provide the sacraments that can prepare the terminally ill for eternal life. This can be the most important blessing we bring to the sick. Many conversions have resulted from Catholics providing spiritual support to the seriously ill. If at first your efforts to convince the sick to receive a priest does not succeed, keep gently trying. Archbishop Fulton Sheen told about a very sick man he visited in the hospital for about fifty days in a row. Every time the Archbishop entered the sick man's room, the man would turn his face to the wall and refuse to talk with his visitor. But the Archbishop kept coming, and no doubt kept praying for the man. Finally, he said to the man that if he would not speak to him, would he at least pray, "Jesus, be merciful to me a sinner!" The man gave no response, and the Archbishop left the room. When the Archbishop returned to the hospital room the next day, a nurse told him the man had died that morning. But she added, "I do not know what you said to him yesterday, but all day long he kept saying, 'Jesus, be merciful to me, a sinner!'"

Redemptive Suffering

Earlier, we touched on co-redemptive suffering and its great value. One very important encouragement we can give to the sick is to unite their sufferings along with their prayers to the sufferings of Jesus. This gives their suffering a great spiritual power, capable of assisting in the conversion of sinners or obtaining graces needed by various members of the Church. Archbishop Sheen always sought the prayers of the suffering, knowing how powerful such prayers were because they were united to the Cross. Suffering can be wasted, however. If people see no good that could come out of their carrying the Cross with Jesus, it may well make them very angry and resentful. As an old saying goes: "Suffering can make you either better or bitter!" But if we point out to the sick that they are carrying the Cross with Jesus and that they can use the merits of their suffering to help others, it can lighten their burden. They may even come to find a certain "joy" in sharing the Cross with Jesus and in suffering for the members of his Mystical Body who need his blessing and mercy most. As the traditional exhortation used for many years during marriage ceremonies puts it: "Sacrifice is difficult and irksome, but love can make sacrifice easy and perfect love can make it a joy."

Assisting the Family of the Sick Person

We also serve the Lord in reaching out to console, encourage, and assist family members and friends of the sick and aged. Their need is often great. Those who are close to the sick person have to bear the cross of seeing a loved one in agony, or suffering significant pain, or simply confined to a bed or wheelchair. Remembering when the sick person was in good health and spirits, they can become depressed by seeing their loved one in an apparently hopeless or terminal situation. They need the help of those who can encourage them and cheer them up, and even pray for them and with them.

The Lord Will Remember
What We Have Done for Him

Visiting the sick and the aged is usually done on the basis of individual need, such as one person visiting another. However, we can also become part of a group—such as a parish outreach, hospice, Third Order, or hospital auxiliary. In this way, we can make this work of mercy a regular ministry.

Visiting the sick brings blessings to the sick and visitors alike, whether one visits a relative or friend who is ill, or a shut-in neighbor, or brings Holy Communion to residents in nursing homes and the homebound, or even serves as part of a hospice group ministering to dying cancer patients. Such service to the sick is serving Jesus, and the Lord will not forget the kindness we have shown him. If he will reward even a cup of cold water given in his name, imagine the reward of those who spend hours consoling him in his suffering brothers and sisters. They are like Simon of Cyrene or Veronica with her veil, ministering lovingly to Jesus as he suffers in the sick, the infirm and the aged members of his Mystical Body.

Visit the Imprisoned

When Jesus describes the works of mercy we can do for him by doing them for the least of his brothers and sisters, the last one he mentions is visiting the imprisoned (Mt 25:36). Though mentioned last, it is a very important work of love that Christians are called to carry out, according to their circumstances in life.

Jesus, Prisoner and Liberator

Jesus himself experienced imprisonment. It is traditionally believed that sometime after his arrest Jesus was held prisoner in a detention cell in the house of Caiaphas, the high priest. Our Lord no doubt submitted to this injustice and indignity to set us free with the freedom of the children of God. He was the Messiah, the Suffering Servant, who had come to "proclaim release to the captives . . . to set at liberty those who are oppressed" (Lk 4:18-19; cf. Is 61:1).

Many Saints Suffered Imprisonment

The Apostles

The apostles likewise endured imprisonment and punishment for refusing to stop proclaiming Jesus as the Risen

Lord (Acts 4:3; 5:17ff.). Saint Peter suffered a rather significant imprisonment and miraculous escape, described in Acts 12. King Herod had begun to persecute the Church and killed Saint James, the brother of Saint John, by the sword. Since this was pleasing to the Jews, he arrested Saint Peter.

> And when [Herod] had seized [Peter], he put him in prison, and delivered him to four squads of soldiers to guard him, intending after the Passover to bring him out to the people. So Peter was kept in prison; but earnest prayer for him was made to God by the Church. The very night when Herod was about to bring him out, Peter was sleeping between two soldiers, bound with two chains, and sentries before the door were guarding the prison; and behold, an angel of the Lord appeared, and a light shone in the cell; and he struck Peter on the side and woke him, saying "Get up quickly." And the chains fell off his hands. And the angel said to him, "Dress yourself and put on your sandals." And he did so. And he said to him, "Wrap your cloak around you and follow me." And he went out and followed him; he did not know that what was done by the angel was real, but thought he was seeing a vision. When they had passed the first and second guard, they came to the iron gate leading into the city. It opened to them of its own accord, and they went out and passed on through one street; and immediately the angel left him. And Peter came to himself, and said, "Now I am sure that the Lord has sent his angel and rescued me from the hand of Herod and from all that the Jewish people were expecting." (Acts 12:4–11)

Interestingly, the chains that miraculously fell from the hands and feet of Saint Peter as he was escaping are displayed in the church of Saint Peter in Chains in the city of Rome.

Saint Paul also suffered imprisonment for the sake of proclaiming Christ and his message of salvation. Like Saint Peter, Saint Paul and his companion Silas underwent persecution and a wondrous rescue while in the ancient city of Philippi.

> And when [the magistrates] had inflicted many blows upon [Paul and Silas], they threw them into prison, charging the jailer to keep them safely. Having received this charge, he put them into the inner prison and fastened their feet in the stocks. But about midnight Paul and Silas were praying and singing hymns to God, and the prisoners were listening to them, and suddenly there was a great earthquake, so that the foundations of the prison were shaken; and immediately all the doors were opened and every one's chains were unfastened. (Acts 16:23–26)

Through these experiences, the apostles not only shared in the suffering of Christ imprisoned, but also the foretaste of his promise of liberty to the captives.

Saint Ignatius of Antioch

Saint Ignatius of Antioch (d. 107) suffered ill treatment from many Roman soldiers who were assigned to escort him by ship from Antioch in Syria to Rome, where he was to be thrown to the lions. Despite the harshness of his imprisonment, however, he did enjoy the consolation of large groups of Christians greeting him at the various ports of call along his journey to Rome. He also took advantage of his opportunity to travel to write letters to various local church communities through which he passed. These letters are extremely important witnesses to life in the early Church. One of the most memorable quotes from the letters of Saint Ignatius was his plea to the Christians in Rome not to intervene to spare his life from martyrdom: "The only thing I ask of you is to allow me to offer the libation of my blood to God. I am the wheat of God, and am ground by the teeth of the wild beasts, that I may be found the pure bread of God."[1]

Saint Felicity

During her imprisonment, the martyr Saint Felicity (d. 203) offered a powerful witness of Christian courage. While in prison, she gave birth to a daughter. When she cried out from the pangs of childbirth, one of the guards taunted her, asking how she would endure the sufferings of martyrdom if she found childbirth so painful. She responded that when she gave birth, she suffered alone; but when she would endure the sufferings of martyrdom, another—Christ himself —will be suffering within her. He would be her strength and consolation in her last agony.

Saint Thomas More

Saint Thomas More (d. 1535) spent fifteen months imprisoned in the famous Tower of London before being executed on false charges of treason, dying, as he said, "the King's good servant but God's first". His imprisonment was a powerful example of steadfast loyalty to the Catholic faith.

Saint Maximilian Mary Kolbe

Saint Maximilian Mary Kolbe (d. 1941), a Conventual-Franciscan priest, spent his imprisonment in the Nazi con-

[1] Alexander Roberts, ed., Sir James Donaldson, ed., and Arthur Cleveland Coxe, comp., *The Ante-Nicene Fathers* (Buffalo, N.Y.: The Christian Literature Publishing Co., 1885), p. 75.

centration camp at Auschwitz serving his fellow prisoners, especially by secretly hearing their confessions late into the night. He culminated his heroic service with the supreme act of love, giving his life for a fellow prisoner who had been condemned to die. He literally fulfilled the words of Jesus: "Greater love has no man than this, that a man lay down his life for his friends" (Jn 15:13).

Saint Pachomius

One saint whose imprisonment stands out is Saint Pachomius (d. 348). He is considered the founder of cenobitic, or community-style, monasticism in the Western Church, as distinct from the eremitical life of hermit monks who lived alone. Saint Pachomius did not suffer imprisonment for his faith. Rather, he found his faith through his experience of imprisonment. From what we know of him, he lived in Egypt, and his family was not Christian. As a young man, he was forcibly drafted into the Roman army along with other recruits. When they rebelled, they were imprisoned. One can only imagine the terrible conditions that prevailed in military prisons in ancient Roman times, but Christian men and women brought food, clothing and other necessities to these prisoners. Pachomius was so impressed by the kindness of these Christians that he decided to become one when he left the army. Later on, he became a monk and founded ten monasteries for men and, with the help of his sister, two monasteries for women in the desert of Egypt. His experience illustrates two important truths: first, that God's grace can produce great conversions even in prisons, and second, that visiting the imprisoned is a powerful tool for evangelization.

Imprisonment: Curse or Blessing

Imprisonment can be one of the most difficult of all crosses to bear. It involves the loss of personal freedom as well as the stigmatizing of the individual with shame for the wrong-doing for which he was incarcerated. It usually means an extended separation from family and friends and in a number of cases, abandonment altogether by loved ones. There is grave danger of exposure to further bad influences from other inmates, and a sense of hopelessness that can lead to despair of God's mercy and the grace to amend their lives. Yet, despite all of these dangers and difficulties, imprisonment has been a "blessing in disguise" for many men and women who, like Saint Pachomius, have experienced the grace of God and profound conversion in their prison cells. To realize this blessing, they need the support of others who love them and care about them. After all, that person in prison could easily have been anyone of us: "There but for the grace of God go I!" Archbishop Sheen, when he would speak to groups in prison, would often say: "The only difference between you and me is that you got caught and I didn't!"

The Right Attitude

Before I made my first visit to a prison as part of a program called REC (Residents Encounter Christ), I had a negative attitude toward prisoners and prison life. Having had no previous contact with prisoners and not thinking much about their situation, I believed prisoners were people who got caught doing wrong, and are now paying their debt to society. But that first visit opened my eyes. The prisoners I met were simply ordinary people who had made their mistakes but were now trying to better themselves. They were attending the REC in order to find God's grace in their lives.

I remember making another visit to a prison to show a film on Saint Padre Pio and give a talk about him. The hosting group was a Holy Name Society within the prison which was well-organized and even printed their own newsletter. These prisoners were openly enthusiastic about the saintly priest who bore the wounds of Jesus. Their response was the same as most other people who had seen the film and heard the talk. Though they lived a far different life from those in a parish group, for example, these were not fundamentally different people or evil people but rather, ordinary people. I would venture to presume that, like most other groups of ordinary people, there were good and bad among them.

In many instances, as we have seen already, imprisonment can give individuals an opportunity to experience conversion. I recently said Mass in a youth correctional facility where a number of lay people carry on a program of spiritual assistance to young men ages eighteen to thirty. Those young men who were Catholics already were learning about their Faith and receiving the sacraments regularly. Others were receiving instructions on the Catholic Faith leading to baptism. There was genuine piety among them. They prayed together, especially the Rosary, with a noticeable fervor. They actively participated in the Holy Sacrifice of the Mass. They sincerely went to confession, too! One young man who came to confession to me was holding a yellow folder in his hands. Before he began to confess his sins, he opened the folder. There, to my pleasant surprise, was a copy of one of my books, *The Gift of God: The Holy Spirit*!

As he handed it to me to sign, he apologized, saying, "I am sorry, Father, that I have not finished reading your book yet. I am only up to Chapter 4." I remember thinking to myself, "They even do spiritual reading!" Of course, I signed his book with great delight.

These spiritual benefits probably would have been missing from the lives of these individuals if they were not in prison. We know that God permits all kinds of evil that he might draw good out of it. At the same time, these spiritual benefits would not have been there were there not concerned and loving Christians who arranged for religious services, gave instructions on the Faith, and provided the rosaries and spiritual reading materials. Above all, these volunteers are bringing their love and concern to people separated from family and friends, and who are often discouraged by guilt and, in certain instances, lifelong rejection.

Doing What You Can to Help the Imprisoned

There are special challenges to visiting the imprisoned. Jails and prisons may be located at a distance. And for obvious reasons they have strict regulations; no one can simply walk into a jail and demand to spend time with any of the inmates. There are security checks both for the individual visitors as well as the items they want to bring along (e.g., books, rosaries). One way a person may approach this work of mercy is to find out if there are any groups such as Residents Encounter Christ, and see if one is qualified to join them. Often your own or a nearby parish offers a prison ministry to which you can belong. There are state and national prison outreach organizations with local chapters.

Other Ways to Help

Even if a person were not actually able to go into the prison and deal directly with the prisoners, there are different ways one can make a "visit". One way is to provide religious books, magazines and materials such as rosaries that the men and women in prison need.

Another way is to write to a prisoner, especially one who has no family. This must be done carefully because prisoners can become emotionally attached. When they leave prison they may expect the individual who has written to them to provide for them or maintain a contact which may present serious difficulties. Therefore, letter writing should only be done with prudence and caution. Before attempting to write to a prisoner, a person should talk to someone, such as the prison chaplain, who can provide him with the name of someone who would benefit from such correspondence. The chaplain could even offer some helpful advice on what this particular individual may need. One should always observe a sense of confidentiality and respect for the privacy of the individual prisoner with whom one is corresponding.

Finally, we can always "visit" by our prayers. We may hear about someone going to jail, or read about it in the newspaper, and be moved to pray for that individual. This can be extremely important. Saint Thérèse of Lisieux, at age fourteen, prayed for a hardened prisoner who was condemned to death for murder, but refused to see a priest. She had heard about this situation and even read about it in the newspaper. She prayed for him intensely, offered sacrifices for his conversion, and even had Mass offered for his conversion. Moments before he was executed for his crimes, this prisoner reached up and kissed a crucifix that was in front of him. The Little Flower accepted this as her sign from God that he had heard her prayers for his conversion! One can only imagine how many prisoners, even on death row, were converted to God through the hidden prayers and sacrifices of others!

Papal Examples

Visiting and assisting those in prison gives these individuals an assurance of God's love and care for them. Even the popes have given us good example of this. What an impression the visit of Pope John XXIII made on Christmas Day, 1960, when he went to visit those jailed in the main prison of Rome. Pope John Paul II made a historic visit to that same prison years later to forgive the man who had attempted to take his life. All this reminds us that Jesus did not break the bruised reed nor quench the dimly burning wick (Is 42:3), which was the prophet Isaiah's way of saying God would not reject us in our sinfulness or brokenness. In fact, our Lord came precisely to heal us and stir our lives into full flame despite our misery and sorrows. We certainly share in Jesus' mission when we reach out and visit those who suffer the loneliness and other hardships of prison life.

Bury the Dead

"To bury the dead" is usually listed as the last of the corporal works of mercy. There are two reasons for this. The first is obvious: the final act of respect we can show to anyone is by burying his mortal remains. All the other corporal works of mercy are shown to the living: the hungry and thirsty, the homeless and naked, the sick and imprisoned. The second reason is that this is the only corporal work of mercy not mentioned by our Lord in his parable of the Last Judgment (cf. Mt 25:34–40). Rather, the Church added this work of mercy out of the respect owed to the human body as "God's temple" (1 Cor 3:16) and out of consideration for the bereaved.

Burial Reflects Belief in the Afterlife

Sacred Scripture states very simply what our human experience confirms: "It is appointed for men to die once" (Heb 9:27). Yet, despite its definitive and mysterious nature, death has been seen in most cultures and civilizations not as a total ending of life, but as a passage into life beyond this world. The ancient Egyptian pyramids, for example, were tombs for the deceased pharaohs and royal family members. Buried along with the deceased were boats needed to "pass over the waters" to the next life, ladders seen as necessary to ascend to where the Deity lived, or even servants to assist these royalty in the afterlife.

Jewish Burial Practice

Burial was the almost universal practice in Israel from earliest times. It involved the committing of the body of the deceased to the ground, usually in a cave or in a sepulcher hewn out of rock. Such places of burial were usually sealed by rolling a large stone across the entrance, as was the case with both Jesus and Lazarus, whom Jesus raised from the dead.

Burial usually took place on the day of death. When death occurred, friends, especially women friends, would hurry to the house of the deceased and begin to make a loud lamentation. Professional mourners would be hired sometimes. The body of the deceased would then be carried on a bier, surrounded by a procession of family members, friends and neighbors, to be interred in its place of burial. An example of this would be the funeral procession for the son of the widow of Nain, whom Jesus compassionately raised from the dead (Lk 7:11–17). Burial was considered extremely important, so much so that even criminals after execution were granted this right. To be deprived of burial was considered a curse.

In earlier Old Testament times, there does not seem to have been any preparation of the body for burial. Closer to the New Testament era, the bodies of the dead were washed; the wealthy would add spices and perfumes and other fragrances, and then wrap the body in linen for burial. As we know from various Gospel accounts (Lk 23:54ff.; Mk 16:1ff.), the body of Jesus, after being taken down from the Cross, was not washed or properly anointed, but because of the approaching Sabbath hastily wrapped in linen and placed in a new tomb. Some of the women, like Saint Mary Magdalene, went to the tomb at sunrise on Easter morning, not expecting to see the Risen Lord, but to anoint his dead body properly.

Early Christian Burial Practice

The care and concern shown for the burial of Jesus was extended to all members of the early Church, which rejected the pagan practice of cremation as contrary to belief in the resurrection. Ananias and Sapphira, who were struck dead by God for lying to the apostles, were nevertheless buried. A group of young men came forward, wrapped up the bodies of each one, and carried them out for burial (cf. Acts 5:1–11). It has been suggested that in the early Church these young men had a ministry of burying the dead. Over time, this ministry became the secular profession of mortician or undertaker.

It is important to mention the great reverence and respect the early Christians had for the martyrs who died in times of persecution. They often were buried in catacombs, which were underground tunnels and rooms with recesses or niches dug as tombs or to hold coffins. These catacombs can still be viewed today, after nearly seventeen hundred years! From the practice of offering the Holy Sacrifice of the Mass near or over the tombs of these martyrs developed the tradition of placing the relics of martyrs in the altar stones used at Mass.

Why Is Burying the Dead a Work of Mercy?

Burying the dead can be seen as a corporal work of mercy in two ways: (1) the sacredness of each person, and in particular of the body, in light of eternal life; and (2) as a time of mourning and farewell. Let us focus our reflections on these two points.

The Body Is Sacred

The body is sacred because it is created by God, made holy by God, and destined for God in the resurrection. In Genesis, after God had created man and woman, he saw that what he had created was "very good" (Gen 1:31). Saint Francis of Assisi offers this thought in one of his admonitions: "Try to realize the dignity God has conferred on you. He created and formed your body in the image of his beloved Son, and your soul in his own likeness."

Furthermore, the body, through the sacrament of baptism, becomes both a "member of Christ", that is, a member of his Mystical Body, and a "temple of the Holy Spirit", who dwells within us (1 Cor 6:15ff.). For these reasons, Saint Paul urges us, "Glorify God in your body."

A final reason why the body is sacred and why we treat it with dignity at death through a respectful burial is because we believe that God will raise our bodies on the Last Day and reunite them with our souls. We will only be complete in our humanity when our bodies and souls are reunited. Our bodies, like that of Christ, will be glorified, so as to share in his eternal glory. Speaking of the body at the time of the resurrection of the dead, Saint Paul writes: "What is sown [buried] is perishable, what is raised is imperishable. It is sown in dishonor, it is raised in glory. It is sown in weakness, it is raised in power. It is sown a physical body, it is raised a spiritual body" (1 Cor 15:42–44).

Burial Is a Time of Mourning and Farewell

Another important purpose for the corporal work of mercy of burying the dead is to assist family and friends in their time of mourning and farewell. No matter how strong we are, we all need physical, emotional and spiritual support to face the great grief and sense of separation that death evokes. This is why the Church's traditional Order of Christian Burial includes a vigil service (wake), the funeral liturgy and the rite of committal. Through this abundance of prayer we celebrate the earthly life of the faithful departed and solemnly honor his passage into eternal life. The ritual brings comfort to the living, and the prayer of the Church unites Heaven and earth, transcending physical separation.

Unless the death of a loved one has been sudden, the grieving process is generally begun even before death takes place. In situations such as a lingering terminal illness or advanced old age, family and friends have an opportunity to express the sentiments of their enduring love, to accept the fact that separation will occur, and even to begin allowing their loved one to leave them. The care given, whether in hospital visits or in regular phone calls, whether in providing for the bodily needs of food and medicine or the spiritual needs of supportive prayer and the sacraments of the Church, is all an expression of love. Many times these acts are also expressions of our gratitude, especially with our own parents. When we were growing up as children, they cared for us; now in their old age, especially when they are nearing the point of death, it is our opportunity to provide the best care we can, personally and through others. As a Sister very dedicated to the elderly once told me: "We enter this life as a child, and we leave this life as a child!"

At the same time, however, watching a loved one's life gradually passing can be a great test of one's faith and love. In the case of those with severe physical or mental suffering, family members and friends must make many acts of faith and trust in God's will and providence that this suffering has a reason, which may not always be apparent. Providing the care needed, as well as sharing the sufferings of loved ones, is all part of the process of letting our loved ones go in death. This can be very important because the dying person may experience feelings of guilt in leaving their loved ones, especially dependents, while those who live on may have feelings of anger at being "abandoned" by one they love. Giving and receiving the "permission" to leave in death may not always be easy, but it is crucial on both sides of the experience of death. The time of mourning assists this process for surviving family and friends, a process which may not be fully realized even for a long period of time after death has taken place.

When the final separation comes suddenly and without warning, as in an accident or tragedy, the time of grief and mourning is extremely important. This is when family and friends need to come together to share their profound sorrow at the sudden loss of a loved one. This is when shared faith and prayer do so much to begin the healing needed after death. Saint Paul reminds us that we must not grieve as those who have no hope (cf. 1 Thess 4:13). Our trust is that our loved ones are with God. We hope someday to be reunited with them in Heaven, where there will be no more suffering, no more separation, where "every tear will be wiped away". These are sentiments we must share with our family and friends in order to have the courage to go on with life.

The wake is the traditional time to bid farewell to our departed loved ones, and to support one another. A wake service usually brings a great deal of comfort for the sorrowing and bereaved, as families and friends instinctively come together in time of sorrow. The funeral Mass and the Rite of Commendation that follow further help the healing, and begin a process of closure.

What about Cremation?

The question of cremation comes up frequently today. In cases where a loved one dies far from the rest of their family, and transportation of the body or proper burial is nearly impossible for various reasons (such as fear of disease), people may seek cremation. The Catholic Church has traditionally forbidden cremation, because in times past it was done to defy the belief in the resurrection of the body, falsely suggesting that not even God can put a body totally burned to ashes back together again. The Catholic Church now permits cremation but still favors a dignified burial. If there are justified reasons (and cost and convenience should not be the sole determining reasons), then cremation is allowed as long as belief in the future resurrection and reverence for the sacredness of the body, even in death, is maintained. If possible, there should be some form of wake and a funeral Mass, and the rules for these differ from one diocese to the next. In all cases, cremated remains must be placed respectfully in a fitting container and reposed in a worthy resting place. Scattering ashes or keeping them in the home are not seen by the Church as showing proper respect for the deceased.

"Life Is Not Ended but Merely Changed"

The Catholic Church considers death an important aspect of life itself. Scripture reminds us that it is appointed that each person has to undergo death. Therefore, death must not be seen as a source of despair as if we were entering into a nothingness. Rather, the Church sees death as a transition from human life in this valley of tears to an eternal life of glory in the Kingdom of Heaven. In one of the prefaces used in the Mass for the Dead, the Church beautifully expresses this truth:

> In him, who rose from the dead,
> our hope of resurrection dawned.
> The sadness of death gives way
> to the bright promise of immortality.
>
> Lord, for your faithful people life is changed, not ended.
> When the body of our earthly dwelling lies in death,
> we gain an everlasting dwelling place in heaven.
> (Preface of Christian Death I)

It is because of our hope in the resurrection, that we continue living with confidence in this life. As Saint Paul observed already in the first Christian generation: "If Christ has not been raised, your faith is futile and you are still in your sins" (1 Cor 15:17). For the Christian everything rests on the reality of Christ's bodily Resurrection. Then we can be sure that he will raise us also on the Last Day. It is no wonder that Saint Augustine rightly called Christians "an Easter people".

THE SPIRITUAL WORKS OF MERCY

Instruct the Ignorant

Catholic theology has always held that our first parents, before the Fall, possessed many gifts from God. Some were
"supernatural gifts" because they gave Adam and Eve certain powers that went beyond or above the capacities of their
human nature. These included the gifts we call "sanctifying
grace" (which is the divine indwelling, or a created share
within the soul of the divine life of the Blessed Trinity);
the theological virtues of faith, hope, and charity; and the
seven sanctifying gifts of the Holy Spirit. They also received
other gifts called "preternatural gifts". These did not go beyond the capacities of human nature, but rather helped to
bring their humanity to a certain fulfillment or perfection.
Among these preternatural gifts were immortality (freedom
from death), integrity (freedom from concupiscence or disordered passions), impassibility (freedom from suffering)
and infused knowledge (an understanding of all things necessary to know without the need of study or instruction).

When our first parents committed the Original Sin, they
lost all these gifts, both supernatural and natural. Jesus came
to restore these gifts to us by his life, death and Resurrection. We have received the supernatural gifts through
baptism, which gave us once again a share in the life of
God in our souls. However, we did not receive back the
preternatural gifts. At the end of our earthly journey, we
will experience bodily death, but with the hope that Jesus

will raise our mortal bodies back to life on the Last Day to share in his glory for all eternity. Because of the loss of the other preternatural gifts, we must struggle with God's grace against the negative effects their loss has caused us. So we struggle against disordered passions (such as anger, lust, and envy) as we strive to practice the opposite virtues. We must bear all kinds of sufferings of body and soul which God uses to purify us from self-love. And finally, we find ourselves today struggling to learn the truths we need to believe and live by in order to enter eternal life. We lost the gift of infused knowledge, by which Adam was able to name all the animals without having studied biology, and instead now we must deal with "confused knowledge", subject to ignorance, error, and falsehood. Our need to acquire truth for ourselves and convey the knowledge of that truth to others is the focus of this spiritual work of mercy.

What Is Ignorance?

Ignorance is a lack of knowledge. For us to learn something, someone must teach us. In the Acts of the Apostles, we find a very good example of how important teaching or instructing another can be. It involves the deacon Philip (Acts 8:26–40) and the story of an Ethiopian court official who was reading the writings of the prophet Isaiah. The deacon Philip, inspired by the Holy Spirit, ran alongside the carriage that the court official was riding in and asked him, "Do you understand what you are reading?" The man answered, "How can I, unless someone guides me?" Then Philip got into the carriage with the man and explained to him that the words of Isaiah referred to Jesus. He went on to explain the full good news about the Lord and ended up baptizing the man. Left to himself, the court official could not understand the Scripture passage he was reading. He needed a teacher to instruct him in the truth.

In the study of philosophy, we say that the human mind at birth is like a blank sheet. In other words, there is no information or data in the mind. We must learn as we grow through life from what we discover through our senses. All of us start off, in a sense, with a certain ignorance; or lack of knowledge; about life itself. Only God does not have any ignorance, rather he has a limitless understanding of all things. Not only does he know the things that actually exist, but he even knows all the possible things that could exist if he were to create them. Human beings, on the other hand, are limited in what they can know. We cannot know all possible things, nor do we have knowledge of everything that exists in the world around us. But there is a kind of required knowledge that is important for each one of us to have. In other words, we certainly need to know those things necessary for our state in life, for our particular living situation and for any employment we may have. What is most important for us, however, is to have a knowledge of those things that are essential to the purpose for which God has created us: namely, to know where we came from, where we are going, and how to get there. These truths are supplied by our Catholic Faith and must be believed and lived in order to carry out our responsibilities to God, to our families, to our neighbors, and even to ourselves.

The Various Kinds and Degrees of Ignorance

If a person were ignorant of the knowledge required of him by his Catholic Faith and by his state in life, this would be a serious form of ignorance since he lacks a knowledge of what he should know. Now, if this essential ignorance results because no one was there to teach him, then his ignorance is one for which he is not responsible. In moral theology, we would call this "inculpable ignorance". However, there is also a "culpable ignorance" that is due to our own fault. Sometimes people want to remain in ignorance deliberately so that they will not know what their responsibilities are. They think that by not knowing them, they are not obliged to carry them out. However, if they deliberately refused to learn about their essential responsibilities, they would be held accountable before God for this ignorance.

Culpable ignorance can also come about through neglect. This happens when persons have an opportunity to learn about their Faith but do not put the proper time and effort into doing so. Such ignorance is hardly bliss, but a kind of prison, holding people back from accomplishing many works of charity and mercy, and developing the talents and gifts that God has given them. As our Lord said in the Gospel, "The truth will make you free" (Jn 8:32).

Ignorance Differs from Error and Falsehood

Of equal concern today with ignorance are error and falsehood. If ignorance is the absence or lack of knowledge, error is mistaken knowledge. Somewhere along the line, persons in error received a knowledge that was not accurate. It did not correspond to reality. Error can have many causes. For example, if a teacher instructing others is in error, that teacher will pass that error along to his students. This error can be passed on in good faith; in other words, the teacher is not aware that what he is saying is not true. This also applies to the sources of knowledge that one uses such as textbooks, materials on the Internet, and the like. If these sources are in error, the one using them will gather knowledge that is unfounded or untrue.

Falsehood is a deliberate distortion of knowledge leading a person to error. Falsehood is basically a deception. It means that what is taught or communicated is deliberately distorted in such a way that someone would not be able to come to a clear and true understanding of things as they really are. Falsehood has a number of causes. It can result if those who are teaching are biased against the truth. Today we talk of people having "personal agendas" in fields of teaching, broadcasting, and the like. Many times, people who push these agendas, such as the "gay" or "radical feminist" agendas, promote values that are in direct conflict with basic Christian values found in the natural law or revealed by God and taught by the Church. An example of this was when the Communists in the Soviet Union would rewrite history, distorting historical facts so as to present the Church and religion in a negative light. This was called "revisionist" history. Such distortions led many people to have a false understanding of what actually happened and to draw incorrect and unfair conclusions. This is especially damaging to the young.

Today we also find agendas in the media, with those who control these influential means of communication often promoting anti-Christian values. They can easily distort the facts by what they say and by what they do not say, or by means of disproportion or failure to provide context. Let me give an example from the sexual abuse scandal in the Church. First, it must be clear that even one case of clerical sexual abuse of a minor is one too many. It cannot be tolerated or excused, but rather condemned. Likewise, the necessary counseling and proper remuneration must be made in each case to try to heal the wounds such horrendous behavior

inflicts on a minor. That being said, there has been an obvious bias in the media in reporting such cases. A few years
ago, for example, there was a news item on the radio that
federal agents had set up a sting operation and had caught
a number of people who were attempting involvement in
pedophilia. The reporter announced that about "twenty-
five people were caught", but only one name was given, the
name of a priest, along with information about the church
he was from. Why was he singled out? This is an obvious example of the stereotyping and profiling of priests that goes
on in the media, resulting in a false notion in many people's minds that "every priest is a pedophile and every pedophile is a priest", even though the vast majority of priests
have never committed such a crime. A priest who was just
standing in a checkout line in a store was approached by a
woman, a total stranger, who asked him bluntly, "Do you
abuse children?" There have been many incidents like this
one throughout the country because a distortion has been
created by the media. Many believe it is intentional, in order
that priests would be discredited, and ultimately the voice
of the Catholic Church would be silenced on moral issues
such as abortion and homosexuality.

Ignorance of the Faith Is Widespread Today

It is a sad fact to admit that ignorance of the Faith is quite
common today among Catholics. People either do not know
their Faith, or have many mistaken notions about it. We experienced a general breakdown in the teaching of the Faith,
especially after Vatican II. The two generations that have
followed since the Council have, in many instances, not received a comprehensive instruction about the Faith. Many
essential doctrinal points were omitted, while simplistic gen-

eralizations abounded. ("The only important thing about Christianity is to be nice to your neighbor.") Add to this the problem of biased teachers who taught what they wanted and not what the Church taught, and the result is a badly informed community of believers. One of the greatest challenges we face is a tremendous need for renewed catechesis in the Catholic Church.

The Proper Formation of Christian Teachers

One way to remedy the problem of ignorance and the even more pressing problems of error and falsehood among Catholic believers today is to form those who will instruct the people in the truths of the Faith. Perhaps we can learn something from the very first catechetical school of the early Church, which was located in Alexandria, Egypt. One of those who headed the school was a Scripture exegete named Origen. He demanded three things of his students: prayer, the "rule of faith", and use of the resources available. Let us look at each of these.

Prayer

First, prayer. It is said that the environment of Origen's school was almost that of a monastic setting. Origen stressed the importance of prayer as necessary to gain the wisdom, understanding, and knowledge of the Holy Spirit that help us to penetrate more deeply into the truths of our Faith and to grasp them more easily so that we can, in turn, teach them clearly to others. Discernment requires the light of the Holy Spirit to help us to distinguish what is truth—what is part of God's revelation and the authentic teaching of the Church, and what is not. Prayer provides an atmosphere that gives us this clarity to understand the truth. Secondly, prayer is needed to live the truth. Archbishop Sheen used to say: "If you do not live what you believe, you will end up believing what you live." It is important that persons live the truth because it then becomes part of them. As a consequence, when they talk about these truths to others, they will speak with the force of personal conviction.

Furthermore, prayer helps us to preserve a clear conscience. This is necessary so that we can grasp the things of the Spirit. Saint Paul says that the "unspiritual man" cannot grasp the things of the Spirit (1 Cor 2:6–16). Why not? He cannot understand spiritual values because he has no appreciation and no attraction for spiritual things. He will therefore remain in a kind of spiritual darkness that will cloud his mind from grasping these truths, not only in their intellectual content, but also as regards the importance of their meaning in his life. Prayer is, therefore, a necessary practice for the true formation of those who will teach the truths of the Faith to others. It was said of many of the early Fathers of the Church that they studied their theology on their knees. They approached theology with reverence, faith, and the desire to receive and share the treasures of the truth contained in these teachings.

The Rule of Faith

The second rule that Origen required was that the theology his students studied had to follow the "Rule of Faith" or in Latin, *Regula Fidei*. This meant that what was taught and what was learned had to be in conformity with true Church teaching. Let me illustrate: If a person were doing simple math, like, two plus two, or two times two, or four ones, or one and three, or three and one, and they arrived at any answer other than four, then this would be a mistake. There would be an error, and if it were deliberate, it would be a falsehood. The same principle applies to what we study and teach to others. This must coincide with what is the actual teaching of the Catholic Church. People have a right to hear the truth, and those who instruct them have a responsibility to teach the truth. We must teach the gospel of Jesus Christ, for this is the "good news" of salvation. We must not teach what we individually prefer, because this would end up being "bad news" for anyone who depended on it to work out their salvation.

Today a lot of people mistake opinion for truth. Popular opinion does not guarantee the truth of an idea, but merely its popularity. Personal opinion reflects what a person feels about a particular issue. Many people today are ready to share their religious opinions without any solid background in, or understanding of, the Faith. Back in the late 1960s, in a seminary classroom one of the students asked his professor, "Can't we dialogue about these aspects of theology?" The professor answered the student, "If I dialogue with you who haven't studied this material, that would be shared ignorance!" So there is an important distinction between opinion and truth; they should not be mistaken for each other.

When we seek the grace of the Holy Spirit, he will give us a gift called the "sense of the faithful". This is a light of the Holy Spirit that helps a person seeking the truth to recognize what is in conformity with Catholic teaching and what is not. Sometimes people have referred to this particular gift of the Holy Spirit in rather humorous ways. Saint Clement Mary Hofbauer, a Redemptorist, used to say: "I have a Catholic nose! I can smell when things aren't the way they should be." In my own seminary studies, certain theological opinions that seemed rather shaky were referred to as "offensive to pious ears". In other words, a person well grounded in the Faith is instinctively disturbed at hearing questionable opinions. This insight from the Holy Spirit helps us remain faithful to the authentic teachings of the Church.

Use Good Resources

Origen's third requirement for his students was that they use the best resources available to gain a deeper understanding of what was being taught, especially Scripture. At the time of Origen this would have included philology, which studies the roots of words and languages as well as the history and customs of the period covered in Sacred Scripture. Origen is credited as being the first teacher in Church history to produce a theological manual or textbook. Today, with so much information available, we still have to seek out the best books, media, videos, Internet resources and other modern means of communication and instruction to prepare those who will teach the gospel message to others. We also need to form teachers in the field of apologetics, which means explaining the Faith to those who have no knowledge of it as well as defending it against those who attack our teachings in any way. We must rely on the Holy Spirit to inspire us to proclaim the truth with a desire to make Christ known and loved by all, and give us the courage to defend the truth. Here is where the influence of the sacrament of confirmation can have a powerful impact on a teacher of the Faith. Through confirmation, the Holy Spirit strengthens us precisely to be adult witnesses of Christ and to be ready to defend our Faith and live it courageously in the face of persecution, ridicule, and rejection.

Another way to form good teachers of the Faith is to come together in study groups where a qualified guide can be instructing many people at the same time. Such communal study and sharing often helps the faithful to understand Church teaching more deeply and to cherish it as the precious gift it is. This is especially helpful in the light of the call to the "New Evangelization" which Pope John Paul II initiated and Pope Benedict XVI has continued to proclaim during his pontificate. Evangelization begins when the individual encounters Christ in a living way. Then, when that person's life has been changed by the encounter, he will want to bring the experience to others. We see an example of this in Scripture with the Samaritan woman's encounter at the well with Christ, who begins to move her toward conversion (Jn 4:5ff.). She immediately goes back into her village and invites all to come out and see the man who "told me all that I ever did!" This new self-awareness prompts her to ask the decisive question, "Can this be the Christ?"

Who Is Called to Instruct the Ignorant?

Everyone should be ready to practice this work of mercy, according to one's ability and situation. It can be formal instruction in a classroom or lecture hall, or simple sharing over a cup of coffee or even in a bar. "Theology on Tap", a program in which young adults gather in a bar for informal discussion on spiritual topics, is popular today. This author even took part in a "Spaghetti and Spirituality" gathering for an older crowd.

Pope John Paul II, in his apostolic exhortation *Catechesis in Our Time*,[1] tells us the responsibility to teach the Faith

[1] Pope John Paul II, *Catechesi Tradendae* (Libreria Editrice Vaticana: 1979). This document may be found at http://www.vatican.va/.

falls on all Catholics, but in different ways according to their different states and positions in life.

The Holy Father first makes reference to his own office as well as that of the bishops as "pastors of the Church", who have the chief responsibility for fostering, guiding and coordinating catechesis. Their role as the Church's supreme teaching authority, the Magisterium, is to expound on Church teaching based on the sources of revelation in Sacred Scripture and tradition. The Magisterium, guided by the gift of infallibility from the Holy Spirit, must preserve the revelation of Christ intact until the end of the world, free from error, heresy, additions, or deletions that would destroy any of its essential truths.

The Holy Father secondly makes reference to the very important role of teaching on the part of parents. Parents lay the groundwork for the religious instruction of their children, and this must serve as the foundation for their whole life of faith. The stronger the foundation, the stronger the faith will remain, and the more the individual can build upon that faith with hope and love. In the ceremony for the baptism of a child, there is a blessing for the parents at the end of the ceremony. In the blessing for the father, the priest says to him:

> God is the giver of all life, human and divine. May he bless the father of this child. He and his wife will be the first teachers of their child in the ways of faith. May they be also the best of teachers, bearing witness to the faith by what they say and do, in Christ Jesus our Lord.

The role of parents is essential to the growth of faith in a child. This is why we look upon the home as the first school of religion and the first church where the child learns to pray. It is also the first Christian community where the child experiences love and witnesses love being given in the works of charity and mercy toward those in need.

The Pope next discusses the preeminent role of priests and religious. Priests teach their parishioners primarily in the homily at Mass and in various forms of instruction, such as adult classes and sacramental preparations. Religious men and women have traditionally exercised their teaching role in Catholic schools and catechetical programs. In this role, priests and religious exercise a powerful influence upon the faithful. Though we live in an age referred to as the "age of the laity", the laity still look to their priests and religious for guidance and encouragement in promoting the gospel message. This has become increasingly important for the challenging mission of the "New Evangelization".

The Holy Father ends with a reference to those who instruct others in the Faith. These include (1) "teachers" who carry out their teaching roles at all levels of education from grammar school to post-graduate studies; (2) "ministers of the Church" who serve in various liturgical functions (e.g., lectors, acolytes) through which they proclaim the word of God; (3) "catechists" whose work, especially in mission countries, not only assists priests and religious but often compensates when they are lacking; and (4) "those in social communications" who have the opportunity to use various media—such as radio, television and the Internet—to reach people who might otherwise not hear the gospel. All of these are true teachers. It is not a matter of one teaching form excluding the others, but rather of all these ministries working together in harmony for the glory of God and the welfare of his Church.

The Dignity and Reward of Instructing the Ignorant

There is great dignity and reward for those who carry out this work of mercy. In the Old Testament we read, "And those who are wise shall shine like the brightness of the firmament; and those who turn many to righteousness, like the stars for ever and ever" (Dan 12:3). Daniel sees that those who have led others into the ways of God will be especially blessed in Heaven. In the New Testament, our Lord reiterates this teaching in the Sermon on the Mount. Speaking about God's law and commandments, he said that they will not be done away with until they are all fulfilled: "Whoever . . . does [these commandments] and teaches them shall be called great in the kingdom of heaven" (Mt 5:19). The results of this important spiritual work of mercy will be to bring many blessings to the People of God on earth and to find a lasting reward with God in Heaven!

Counsel the Doubtful

What Does "Counseling the Doubtful" Mean?

Doubts are a part of life. Everybody experiences them at one time or another. There are the simple doubts that arise daily, everything from "I wonder if I turned off the stove when I left the house this morning?" to "I can't remember if the doctor told me to take my medication with supper or at bedtime?" These kinds of doubts do not need any counseling. Perhaps a phone call to a relative or friend back home or one's doctor could resolve the questions about the kitchen stove and the medication. The kind of doubts that can be relieved as a spiritual work of mercy are those which affect our beliefs about ourselves and who we are in God. Doubt can steal our peace of mind and instill fear and sorrow, but counsel can restore serenity. Let us look at a few of these.

Doubts about Self-Worth

We all have a "self-image", or an internal idea of what we think of ourselves. As we mature in life, through what we learn and experience, this self-image is formed as our understanding of who we are and what we can do. This image serves a very important function as a support for our sense of self-worth. Recognizing our self-worth is key to living our lives with a sound emotional foundation. We have to be able to recognize that God created us as good, that we are special or unique because of his personal love for each of us. He loves us as the individuals we are, and not simply as part of a group. He loves us, furthermore, despite our sins and imperfections, our failures and weaknesses. This self-worth is built up in us by the love and acceptance we receive from others, especially our parents, siblings, other relatives, and friends. Because they love and accept us, we know that we are lovable and acceptable.

But since none of us were raised in a perfect family or with perfect friends, we all have scars that diminish our self-worth. At times, we question our own worth, whether our life has any importance or meaning at all. Counseling people who experience these doubts to a significant degree is very important. Getting them to accept their God-given worth can mean the difference between joy in living and a life filled with self-reproach and self-rejection. Sound counsel will remind people of the truth of a popular saying: "God made me, and God doesn't make junk!"

Doubts about Self-Confidence

What is true about a sense of low self-worth applies also to an individual's sense of self-confidence. Some people throw up their hands in discouragement, frustration, or even anger when facing the tasks and challenges in life even before they have begun to tackle them. They have a defeatist attitude which expresses itself as "I can't do it!" This can become a self-fulfilling prophecy: The task never gets done! These persons need to be encouraged to try their best. As someone once put it, "It is better to fail at trying than to succeed at not trying." Sometimes this kind of paralysis at effort-making has its roots in childhood, if the person was criticized too severely for childish mistakes. Parents, teachers and others who deal with the young need to be able to balance praise with blame, keeping in mind that children need a lot more affirmation than correction. Otherwise, the child may unconsciously absorb a perfectionist attitude: People will only accept whatever I do when it is done perfectly. This easily translates into a compulsive need to try to do everything perfectly in life! As a consequence, fear of failure, of doing something less than perfect, can become an oppressive burden. It will take on an obsessive quality that can turn into a defeatist attitude that locks up self-confidence. Most people realize they do not need to do everything perfectly, but if their store of self-confidence is minimal, they need to hear someone else say that to them. This is a common form of counseling the doubtful. As a person's self-confidence grows, he will reach a point where he can say it to himself. When he does, he will have reached a very important level of emotional and even spiritual maturity.

Someone may question, "How are these instances of counseling 'spiritual works of mercy'? Aren't they simply basic emotional guidance?" There is an important principle in Christian spirituality: Grace builds on nature. Many of the problems we encounter in our spiritual growth are not purely spiritual. They have emotional roots. If we encourage people to grow authentically in their emotional life, they will grow spiritually as well. It is like "dispelling the demons" of discouragement, self-pity, apathy, fear, and despair. This is a genuine work of mercy. We can apply here the words of Saint Elizabeth Ann Seton, "Who can hold back the soul that God sets free?" One of the greatest human freedoms is the freedom from a self-imposed prison of discouragement and fear.

Moral Doubts

People often encounter doubts regarding their moral behavior. Questions about what is morally good or bad, or what is more appropriate for their spiritual growth or for their peace of mind and heart, can distress them. These doubts are more frequent today because of the many distorted opinions and values that abound in secular society and which are in contradiction to the Church's authentic moral teachings. Sometimes, simply explaining the true meaning of the commandments or the teachings of the Church can resolve these doubts. Directing people to read the *Catechism of the Catholic Church* can help immensely. Other doubts may require lengthy counseling to help the person discern truth from falsehood. This is especially important today in the light of the great stress on a personal or subjective view of life: "It may be against the Church teaching, but is it wrong for me to act this way? Don't my circumstances or my situation justify my behavior?" As Archbishop Sheen would say, "If you do not live what you believe, you will end up believing what you live!"

One form of moral doubt that is particularly difficult to deal with is scrupulosity. The word comes from a Latin word that means a very small stone, a pebble. When you get a pebble in your shoe, small though it is, it causes a big annoyance. So, the doubts and fears of a scrupulous person generally concern small matters, but they produce disproportionately big worries and feelings of guilt. A scrupulous person, for example, is inclined to see sin where there is no sin or grave sin where there is only a slight wrong. The basis of scrupulosity is often a fear springing from a rather severe notion of God as judging and condemning harshly even the slightest infractions. This type of person easily becomes obsessed with anxiety over having done wrong (for example, he may examine his conscience continuously over thoughts that come into his mind without his even wanting them), and likewise feels a constant compulsive need to go to confession. Not everyone is qualified to counsel such persons. They need skilled help to remedy their condition. But anyone can offer the simple wisdom of reminding them of God's love, that Jesus died on the Cross to take away their sins. We can encourage them to pray for trust in his mercy and remind them of our Lord's words to Saint Faustina, "Tell the people to focus less on their sins and more on my mercy!" Patience, gentle persistence and prayer is needed in this area of counseling, because doubts arising from an underlying fear are not easily resolved.

Doubts in Spiritual Direction

Qualified people who do spiritual direction frequently practice this work of mercy. The word "qualified" here is important. Guiding another soul requires proper knowledge of how the spiritual life develops as well as an ability to discern the working of the three spirits involved here: the Holy Spirit, the evil spirit, and the human spirit. Without such knowledge and insight, a person can do harm to a soul by misinformation or faulty guidance. Frequently spiritual direction involves resolving serious doubts, especially those caused by the devil's lies or by our own "deceitful lusts" (Eph 4:22). Anyone can give basic spiritual advice, such as Saint Padre Pio's famous quote, "Pray, trust and don't worry!" But if there appear to be more serious concerns, advising a person to see a good priest or other spiritual director is itself a work of mercy.

Doubts in Life Situations

Life itself is filled with decisions and challenges that cause doubts and uncertainty. As we try to cope with them, we may realize that we can benefit from guidance or advice from others. Perhaps one is discerning a vocation in life ("I am attracted to this particular person and feel led to marry this individual. Do you think she is the right person for me?") Or one could be facing a choice of a career or problems with family members or friends ("I seem to be always arguing with my parents", or "I am having a lot of tension with a certain person at work. What can I do?") Maybe the counsel needed is direct advice, such as "If your parents' anniversary is coming up soon, send them a card and tell them you love them. That can start better communication going", or "If you feel secure enough with that person at work, ask him to meet with you over lunch or a cup of coffee. Talk over your feelings without blaming the other person and try to arrive at a solution." This counsel may seem simple, but people stuck in their difficulties often miss even the most obvious solutions.

There are many other instances when doubts are encountered. They usually can and should be resolved, as far as humanly possible, with the grace of God. What a great act of mercy it is to help others resolve their doubts. Removing these negative thoughts that weigh heavily on the minds of our brothers and sisters in faith can free them to live more fully the life God has given them with the dignity and peace they should have as his sons and daughters.

Admonish the Sinner

Vince Lombardi, considered by many the greatest football coach of all time, coached the Green Bay Packers to win the first two Super Bowls. He is known for many popular sayings, including the famous line: "Winning isn't everything; it's the only thing." I often paraphrase that saying: "For the Christian, salvation isn't everything, it's the only thing!" Jesus himself tells us that if we were to gain the whole world yet lose ourselves in the process, in the end we have gained nothing (Lk 9:25). In fact, we will have missed the very purpose for which God created us, namely, to share eternal life with him in the Kingdom of Heaven. The greatest obstacle to our salvation is sin. Therefore, the Christian must be ready to resist sin in himself at any cost and, at the same time, be willing to help others to resist sin in their own lives as well.

We Need to Admonish Ourselves First

To admonish the sinner begins by admonishing oneself. After all, we are all sinners. Humility is the virtue by which we recognize our sinfulness and weakness. As a result, we realize that we depend upon God's mercy to forgive us our past sins and upon his grace to strengthen us to resist sin in the future. Without humility, we will not admit our sins honestly to ourselves and, when needed, to others. Since human weakness is always present due to Original Sin and our own past personal sins, we must struggle each day to resist evil and do good. The Bible says that even a righteous man falls seven times (Prov 24:16). In biblical terms "righteous" means "holy". So even the saints had their sins and needed to remind themselves constantly of the danger of sinning. They needed always to beware of falling again. Jesus himself told the apostles in the Garden of Gethsemane, "Watch and pray that you may not enter into temptation" (Mt 26:41). When we "watch", we are vigilant to avoid the occasions of sin, namely, any person, place, or thing that would lead us to offend God. When we "pray", we strengthen ourselves to resist sin by asking God for the grace to carry out his will every day.

To admonish others effectively, there are three points to keep in mind. First, we must practice what we preach. In other words, we have to be striving for holiness and avoiding sin in our own lives if we expect others to do the same. It has been said, "I can't hear what you are saying because what you are doing speaks so loudly." Our words will have the force of conviction only if we ourselves follow them.

The second point is to avoid the terrible attitude of self-righteousness with its judgmental view of others. Self-righteousness puts a person in the mindset of the Pharisees who were quick to condemn sin in others but overlooked it or easily excused it in themselves. This was the point of Jesus' challenge to them in the Gospel story of the woman caught in adultery (Jn 8:3ff.). The Pharisees were quite ready to condemn this woman for her sin. In fact, they tried to put Jesus on the spot as to whether the woman should be stoned or not, according to the law of Moses. Jesus did not say "yes", nor did he say "no". He simply threw the challenge back at them: "Let the one among you who has no sin cast the first stone." The Gospel then tells us he began to write on the ground. Whatever he wrote apparently referred to each individual's sins because as each one saw what our Lord wrote, he dropped his stones and walked away. To carry out the work of admonishing a sinner, a person must have compassion for human weakness, and we can only develop that by recognizing our own weaknesses. If we fail to do so, we will be throwing a lot of stones at other people and in the process condemning ourselves.

Another important point follows from this. It comes from the teaching of Saint Paul who wrote that "in passing judgment upon [others] you condemn yourself" (Rom 2:1). This is not only a wise spiritual counsel, but it is also an important insight into human psychology. If we do not acknowledge our own faults, we will most assuredly see these same faults glaring at us in our neighbors. We will probably condemn these faults mercilessly in them, like the Pharisees with their stones, ready to punish the woman caught in adultery. Why do we act this way? It is because we are really angry at having these faults ourselves, but since we don't acknowledge them in ourselves we unconsciously transfer our anger onto other people in whom we see these same faults. In correcting the faults of another person, we must be careful to avoid unjustified anger or harshness. Otherwise, the cure administered will end up doing more harm than the fault needing correction.

Admonishing a Sinner May Mean His Salvation

The basic reason that we admonish sinners is because their salvation may be in jeopardy, and their salvation is their greatest good and need. If a person were drowning and we were standing near a life preserver, but failed to throw it to that person so that he could be saved, this would be a terrible act of omission. It would be even worse if a soul were in jeopardy of eternal loss from God, and we said or did nothing when we could make that person realize the moral danger he is in. Greater than all our bodily needs is the spiritual need to be set free from sin and receive the life of God. This is why admonishing a sinner is so important. Saint Francis of Assisi used to say that nothing should take precedence over the work of the salvation of souls. It was for this reason that he was so ardent in prayer for the conversion of sinners, why he preached so earnestly and sincerely calling people to repentance, and why he always strove to give a good example of Christian life, that he might move others to know and love God more. In the Acts of the Apostles (6:2), we read how the apostles would not abandon their work of prayer and preaching the word of God to serve widows at tables, not because they disdained the work of serving at table, but because they realized it was more important for them to serve the spiritual food of the word of God, calling people to conversion and to his mercy, than even to feed their bodies. We too must have a deep sense of compassion and concern for the salvation of others.

Despite its great importance, admonishing sinners is a difficult and dangerous work of mercy because people do not like to be reminded of their sins and faults. None of us likes to be corrected. It goes against the grain with us; it stings us to hear that we have done something wrong. This is even more so if the person has entered into a denial of sin in his life. Pope John Paul II has said that one of the greatest difficulties we face in the world today is the loss of a sense of sin. We used to say years ago that something was "as obvious as sin". Sin is far from obvious today with many people. Archbishop Sheen would say that 150 years ago, when the Catholic Church declared the Immaculate Conception of the Blessed Virgin Mary, there were many people who were up in arms that the Church would dare say that there was even one person without sin. Now, he said, everybody is without sin! So if people are forgetful or in denial, which is even worse, they will very probably react badly if they are reminded of their sins. This reaction is very common outside of abortion clinics when pro-life advocates try to dissuade women from going in and having abortions. Sometimes the women themselves, or family members, or especially boyfriends who escort them into the abortion clinics, will react with rage and abusive language because those who are praying or counseling are reminding them of the evil of what they are really doing in taking the life of the unborn.

Proceed with Great Caution but Proceed

To admonish anyone about his sins certainly is a very delicate matter. Because of the possibility of stirring up anger and resentment, one must approach the person with care and sensitivity. There are things we can say, and there are other things perhaps best left unsaid for the moment. Dorothy Day used to say: "Jesus came for two reasons: he came to comfort the afflicted and afflict the comfortable." If you admonish certain sinners, you will afflict them. Therefore, we must proceed with compassion and a sense of humility, and never try to confront people with an attitude of self-righteousness: "I am better than you are", or "I'm here to correct you." The difficulty, as we have seen, lies in the fact that no one likes to be reminded of his sins. Jesus says in the Gospel of Saint John (3:19–21) that men do evil deeds in darkness, so as not to be exposed. The light of truth stings their consciences, or at least hurts their pride and vanity.

This work of mercy is made more difficult today by a general attitude that we should never "judge anyone". However, we must make an important distinction when it comes to judging the morality of people's actions. If an action is wrong, if it is a sin, we must condemn it. On the other hand, we do not condemn the sinner but try to encourage that person to repentance and conversion. After all, no one hated sin more than Jesus, and yet no one loved sinners more than Jesus! In spite of the difficulties, however, we must be willing to risk trying to win people over from their sinful ways. If they are sincere, in the end they will thank us. Jesus says that those who are sincere will welcome the light to verify the truthfulness and goodness of their deeds. In other words, being sincere, they will welcome the light of someone pointing out where they may be doing wrong because they probably are unaware of it or of any harmful effects their actions may have in this life or in the next. You actually will set them free by pointing out their sins, even if at first they may resist your attempts to do so.

A famous story in the life of Archbishop Sheen illustrates this well. As a young priest, he was on duty at Saint Patrick's Church in Soho Square in London. An actress came to the rectory to speak with a priest about her rather sinful life. However, to get up the courage to do so, she drank quite a bit. As young Father Sheen tried to speak to her about her immoral living, it was apparent that because she drank so much, she could not understand what he was saying to her. So he asked her, "Would you come back and see me when you are feeling better?" She answered, "Yes, but on one condition: that you promise me you will not ask me to go to Confession!" Father Sheen promised her. In fact, he promised three times in all: twice before she left and once when she came back! When she returned in a sober state, they spoke for about an hour and she felt much better. As she was ready to leave, he said to her, "Can I show you the inside of our Church? We have some very beautiful paintings there." She agreed, and as they were walking along the side aisle, they came by the confessional, and he pushed her right in. He kept his promise: He did not ask her to go to confession! The woman made a confession of her whole life, and later on became a cloistered nun for more than forty years in nearby Tyburn Convent in London. When the woman kept saying, "Promise me you will not ask me to go to confession", young Father Sheen realized that she was really unconsciously yearning to go to the sacrament of God's mercy! She was protesting too much, and it became evident that what she really needed and wanted was God's forgiveness.

Ways to Admonish the Sinner

If we look up the word *admonish*, we will find it has various meanings, which indicate different ways we can carry out this spiritual work of mercy. Let us reflect on these different meanings.

To admonish a sinner means, first of all, to call someone to conversion. Jesus himself did this from the very outset of his public ministry when he proclaimed, "the kingdom of God is at hand; repent and believe in the gospel" (Mk 1:15). We can call people to conversion in different ways. Sometimes it comes by formal preaching, such as at a parish mission or a retreat, or maybe in a witness talk of one's own conversion story. Another way is in a one-on-one talk or a small group discussion. Even yet another call can be non-verbal, simply by the good example of refusing to participate in wrongdoing. Good example has a great witness power.

Another way to admonish is to inform or remind someone by way of a warning of the moral danger they are in. Priests and parents often practice this form of admonishing. It focuses on a specific individual in need of this warning. For example, Saint Padre Pio once warned a man in the confessional to change his lifestyle because he was in danger of going to Hell. When the man said that he did not believe in Hell, Padre Pio told him he would believe in Hell when he got there! We can be sure the man got the message.

Cautioning a person to correct certain specific faults is another form of admonishing. Some people have an obligation in justice to do this by their very office or authority. For example, a bishop in his diocese must correct blatant evils, a superior of a religious community must correct abuses, a spiritual director must correct those receiving his direction, and parents must correct their children. It is important to remember in these instances that the correction given must be aimed at making the erring person do better rather than making the correcting person feel better. This means that corrections should not be given out of anger or annoyance. For example, Saint Francis in his Rule directed those in authority to "visit and admonish their brothers, and humbly and charitably correct them".[1] When giving a penance to an erring friar they "must be careful not to be angry or disturbed at the sin of another, for anger and disturbance

---

[1] Francis of Assisi, *The Later Rule (1223)*, in *Francis of Assisi: Early Documents*, vol. 1, *The Saint*, ed. Regis J. Armstrong, O.F.M. Cap. (Hyde Park, N.Y.: New City Press, 1999), p. 105.

impede charity in themselves and in others".[2] Parents, too, need to be careful of correcting with extreme anger when they are annoyed by their children's faults, for such anger can easily lead to verbal and even physical abuse.

Another form of admonishment is fraternal correction. This is considered an expression of charity. Out of love and concern for a brother or sister in Christ, one brings to their attention faults or shortcomings that may be harming the individual or negatively affecting others in a family or community. True friends would want to do this for one another. A caution here is to avoid pettiness in matters that one corrects. Many shortcomings do not affect others negatively and should therefore be borne patiently. This kind of admonishing many times involves nothing more than a mild reproof as, for example, for laziness or indifference on the part of someone who should have helped out.

A final form of admonishing sinners is to encourage and even urge them on to greater efforts, or to persevere in their struggle to break from a life of sin. This form of admonishment is directed to persons who are weak and fall often, or to the fainthearted who fear the price of the effort needed to reform their lives, or to the lukewarm who lack a zealous motivation and a firm determination to change their lives.

Silence in the Face of Evil Is Disastrous

There is an old saying, "All that is needed for evil to succeed is for good people to say or do nothing." Silence in the face of evil allows that evil to continue and even to spread. Such a terrible silence must be broken. To paraphrase one of Archbishop Sheen's famous quotes, "We don't need a

[2] Ibid., p. 104.

voice that's right when everybody else is right; but we need a voice that's right when everybody else is wrong." This is especially applicable to those in positions of responsibility for guiding others. Sacred Scripture, for example, contains certain images for those in leadership among God's people. They are to be like shepherds (Jn 10:1ff.) guarding their sheep, ready even to lay down their lives to protect their sheep from harm. If they remain silent, they are simply running away like hired hands in the face of danger. Elsewhere they are compared to watchmen in their towers, guarding the city from attack (Ezek 33:1ff.). If they see the enemy coming and sound the alarm, the city will be defended; but if they fail to do so, all will be lost. Finally, Saint Gregory the Great uses the image of the watchdog that guards against thieves and other intruders. But, he says, if the watchdog cannot bark, it is useless!

Parents must also fulfill their responsibilities as best they can. Disciplining children in an appropriate way may save both children and parents from a lot of future grief and sorrow. As the old proverb wisely teaches, "Spare the rod and spoil the child." The "rod" here would be better understood as a proper correction or verbal discipline rather than simply a form of physical punishment. Even fraternal correction, given early enough and lovingly enough, can make a big difference. It can serve as a clear light during a moment of serious darkness in a person's life.

Admonishing Sinners Merits a Great Reward

Saint James in his letter (Jas 5:19–20) tells us that there is a great reward in store for those who help a sinner find his way to Christ. They will save the soul of the erring brother in Christ and at the same time cover a "multitude" of their own sins, because God will be merciful to them for their work of mercy to another. We should ask God to give us a fervent desire for the salvation of souls. Great saints and mystics who write about the spiritual life assure us that this desire is something that grows intensely as one draws closer to God. This desire will strengthen the conviction to admonish those who need it, even when the task is challenging. In this way, we will help satisfy the deep thirst of Jesus upon the Cross for the salvation of all men and women for whom he laid down his life.

Bear Wrongs Patiently

To bear wrongs patiently is by no means easy. Whether the wrongs we suffer are severe or simply minor annoyances, most of us are inclined to complain, to react, or even to strike back. The story is told about a truck driver who was having a meal in a small diner about two o'clock in the morning. He was the only person in the diner besides the cook. He was peacefully enjoying his meal when suddenly three members of a tough motorcycle gang came into the diner. They were itching for trouble and wanted to provoke this big truck driver into a fight. Each one of them did what he could to get him angry. The first one threw the truck driver's hat on the floor and stepped on it. The second one threw his cigarette in the truck driver's cup of coffee. The third one even took his plate of food, turned it upside down, and threw it on the counter, splattering food everywhere. Despite all of these things, the truck driver didn't react at all. Without saying a word, he simply picked up his hat and walked out the door. The members of the motorcycle gang were absolutely amazed at the truck driver's lack of response. The leader of the gang said, "Did you see that? That guy is not much of a man, not much of a man at all!" Just then, the cook was looking out the window and he said, "Yeah, and he's not much of a truck driver either. Pulling out of here he just drove over three motorcycles!" The truck driver didn't bear the wrongs patiently after all. He simply lived by the principle "I don't get angry; I just get even." While we can understand why people desire to get even, Jesus asks us to respond differently.

Suffering Wrongs Is a Fact of Life

We all experience hardships that seem unfair. Most of the wrongs we suffer are caused by people around us, but others simply come from situations in life. We need to look at how to bear both kinds of wrongs patiently.

The Wrongs That Come from Life Situations

Some wrongs in life come from situations over which we have little or no control and which no one intends. They can happen at any time and in any way, and they can involve things that are very simple or very serious. For example, something is misplaced that we need immediately, and even Saint Anthony does not answer our prayer to find it right away. Or there is an electrical power outage just when we are about to save an important file on the computer. Then there are the everyday trials at the job, at school, or even in the parish. Still other difficulties can arise if our plans are disrupted or go awry, as when a scheduled flight to visit family members is canceled because of bad weather. Some difficulties are more serious in their consequences—a teenage son getting involved in an accident leading to serious injury, a sickness that causes lasting physical or emotional health problems, or a loss of one's job. Many of us hope that our dreams will come true, but sometimes our nightmares come true also. We must learn to deal with these situations, to accept them, and to work through them. As the saying goes,

"When you get lemons in life, make lemonade." However, if our best efforts fail, we may have to be resigned to that fact. We must try to bear these "wrongs" patiently. We do this by accepting with trust in God the things that he permits to happen which we cannot change.

The Wrongs That Come from Other People

Most of the wrongs we experience come from other people. Depending on the wrong done or the wrongdoer, our annoyance level will measure higher or lower. For example, others can wrong us with little slights that offend us, especially if we are sensitive. Maybe someone takes us for granted, or treats us with a matter-of-fact attitude instead of friendliness. Another person fails to help us in a small matter when the need for help was obvious. Sometimes the wrongs can be sharper, as when people are rude to us. How do these things make us feel? Do we think, "What am I, chopped liver?" These feelings can be even more intense if people insult us by deliberately showing us contempt. We know that the Lord himself was insulted in this way by the Pharisees during his public ministry. When he was on trial, they slapped him and even spit at him. Obviously, these were terrible wrongs. The Lord had the power, with one thought of his mind, to eliminate his enemies from the very face of the earth, but he gave us the example of bearing these wrongs patiently.

No doubt one of the hardest wrongs to bear is a betrayal by someone with whom we have had a bond of trust. Again, we need only think of the example of Jesus' betrayal by Judas. Our Lord even said to Judas as he was about to turn him over by an act of apparent love and friendship, "Judas, would you betray the Son of man with a kiss?" (Lk 22:48).

Many of the wrongs that come from other people, however, come through thoughtlessness. They are not deliberately intended, but they still cause us irritation. In such cases we must learn patience to die to our self-love. We need to deal with our hurt feelings without undue anger or reacting in a manner that would betray our love for Christ. Needless to say, for many of us it takes much practice before we can perform this spiritual work of mercy.

Our Comfort Zone

The wrongs that others commit against us may be attitudes or actions that simply get on our nerves. Saint Thérèse, the "Little Flower", often felt an annoyance with a Sister in her community who constantly clicked her teeth in the chapel. This affected Thérèse's meditations and certainly must have gotten on her nerves. What she did, however, was to turn the noise of the Sister clicking her teeth into a "little song", a kind of melody that she offered to Almighty God. Obviously, Saint Thérèse was a great saint! She practiced heroic virtue, even though this particular difficulty seemed so small and insignificant. A lot of people would certainly have taken another course of action. They might well have "lost their cool"!

The distress or agitation we feel from these wrongs is due to the disruption of our comfort. We all have a "comfort zone" around us that we try to protect with an unseen sign saying, "Do not disturb!" This comfort zone includes our private time, our convenience, and our preferences. We like to keep people out of that zone. When people disrupt our privacy and enter into our comfort zone by making demands on our time, attention, or service, we will feel annoyed at them. For example, just when we have our time already planned out in terms of what we are going to do, someone unexpectedly comes along who needs our help or attention. This is a needy brother in Christ who has come, or perhaps we can say it is Christ who comes in a needy brother. As Mother Teresa would remind us often, "Jesus comes in the distressing disguise of the poor." And when he comes at a time when we had other plans, it can be extremely distressing. It's like living with Murphy's Law: "If anything can go wrong, it will, and at the worst possible moment." It takes a great deal of patience to accept people and situations that are unexpected, or inconvenient, or irritating.

Those Who Make Our Burdens Heavier

Other wrongs come from those who make life unnecessarily difficult. Unlike the people we just mentioned, who make demands on our convenience or disturb our comfort, these people affect us by their thoughtlessness, laziness, and even negligence of duty. This means that, many times, we end up having to clean up after them. Their carelessness makes a lot of extra work for a lot of other people. Usually we experience varying degrees of anger toward these people. We might even react: "Who needs these people?" It is precisely at these moments that Jesus would say to us, "You do, and that is why I sent these people to you." It's precisely these kinds of people who help us to grow in patience. They are included in people Jesus speaks of when he says, "Love your enemies" (Mt 5:44). By "enemies", Jesus means those we must struggle to love. But if we didn't have these kinds of people in our lives, our love would never grow beyond the comfortable stage. These people force us to give a great deal more if we are to love them the way Jesus loves us. This kind of love is at the heart of the gift of mercy and, in turn, at the very heart of the gospel message that we must love one another because God has loved us. Jesus gave us a new commandment: "Love one another as I have loved you" (Jn 15:12). He even goes further: "Be perfect, as your heavenly Father is perfect" (Mt 5:48). If you think this is very difficult, or even humanly impossible, you are right. It can only be done with the help of God's grace and following the example of Jesus, who said, "Learn from me; for I am gentle and lowly in heart" (Mt 11:29). To do this, we must deal with our impatience and our anger.

Dealing with Our Impatience

Impatience is a slight irritability that we show when people annoy us. One good way of being prepared to resist the impulse to impatience is to pray often the little "Serenity Prayer": "God, grant me the patience to accept the things I cannot change, the courage to change the things I can, and the wisdom to know the difference."

We need the virtue of patience to deal with those brothers and sisters who make us feel irritated or offended. One important thing we can do is to give a little space to those persons to be themselves, as we would want them to respect the space we need to be ourselves. Nitpicking or fault-finding with them is certainly not helpful. Always remember that they have to put up with us, and that is not always the easiest thing for them to do, either. I myself think about this point often. When someone seems to irritate me, I say "Well, I've got to put up with him." Then the thought dawns on me, "They have to put up with me, too!" So give room to others to be imperfect, and to grow, as we would want to have this room for ourselves.

Change What You Can

Another way to deal with our impatience is to follow the part of the Serenity Prayer that says, "Change the things you can." One important way to do this is by open and honest communication. If we tend to store up all our feelings about the little things that irritate us, we might one day "explode" by blowing up at someone. Or we might "implode" by getting very depressed with pent-up anger submerged deep within us. When we have good communication, we can more easily dispel the irritation due to misunderstanding. I remember the story of a husband and wife who were having problems in their marriage, so they went to see a marriage counselor. The counselor asked the husband, "What is it that you find most difficult about your wife?" The husband answered, "She is always cooking string beans, which I can't stand." The wife blurted out, "But honey, I thought you loved string beans! That's why I made them so often for you!" Good communication would have resolved the source of irritation and probably years of tension in their marriage.

Detachment

Another factor that can help us to have patience is learning to be somewhat detached so that we do not cling too tightly to things, such as material possessions. They are not worthy of our esteem if they are going to cause us to offend our neighbor. Jesus did not die to redeem material things, but to redeem our neighbor and us. He poured out his Precious Blood for the salvation of others as well as for us. Therefore, with a sufficient amount of detachment, we can let go of things, such as material items, or even our own opinion, when these are not necessary to hold onto! Archbishop Sheen used to say, "I would rather lose a thousand arguments than one soul." Or, to put it another way, "Don't make a mountain out of a molehill."

Cheerfulness

A proven method to overcome impatience and irritability is to foster a spirit of generosity and cheerfulness. Jesus says in the Gospel, "You received without pay, give without pay" (Mt 10:8). Everything that we possess in life is truly a gift of God to us. It is in a sense lent to us in this life. Therefore, we should be ready to let these things go in a reasonable way when we need to help our neighbor. Certainly, God will never be outdone in generosity. When we share what God has given us, we are being good stewards of these gifts because they are not ours to possess forever, but ours to share with others and to use in an appropriate way to help those who are less fortunate than ourselves.

Be Compassionate

We must also be compassionate, meaning to feel what another is going through. Sometimes a person may be having a bad day or has just come through a very difficult trial, and without realizing it, thoughtlessly passes negativity on to us. By means of compassion we should try to understand what that person may be feeling, and this can help us to put a lid on our feelings of anger. We must also be forgiving, just as God has forgiven us in Christ. Remember our own sins, and we will be much more compassionate with the sins of others. It is when we forget that God has forgiven us and has been patient with us, that we will be harsh towards others.

We are given the opportunity, through bearing patiently the wrongs of others, to show the Lord how grateful we are for his kindness to us. This is where the virtue of meekness is very important. Meekness is rooted in charity and gives us the strength to stand calmly in the face of injustice, irritation, or provocations of various kinds, and to not give way to natural feelings of anger and resentment. We need an interior peace and serenity of spirit in order to practice the virtue of meekness. One thing we certainly must not do is hold on to past thoughts of injustice and mistreatment. Saint Paul reminds us: "Be angry but do not sin; do not let the sun go down on your anger, and give no opportunity to the devil" (Eph 4:26–27). What the Apostle is saying here is that if we hold on to anger and "stew" overnight from one day to the next, at some point the devil will turn that anger against our spiritual good. He will stir us up to a point of uncharitableness toward our neighbor. This is why we should try to resolve our anger as quickly as possible and not let it linger. And part of the forgiving is forgetting.

Jesus' teaching on loving our enemies applies here. If we merely tolerate the hurt or loss that we suffer, we probably will resent it bitterly. A festering memory of anger will lodge in our hearts. But if we overcome the repulsive aspect of the wrong or harm done to us, we begin to transform anger into the virtue of meekness. As Saint Paul told the Romans, "Do not be overcome by evil, but overcome evil with good!" (Rom 12:21). A transformation can occur as we go from anger and resentment to the beginning of patience by bearing with the wrong that is done. We can then move beyond simple patience to an acceptance of what God has permitted this person to do to us. This becomes a kind of resignation to the situation, especially when either we cannot remedy the situation or it would cause us to resort to violence or vengeance as a means of trying to exact justice. From this kind of resignation and acceptance we can move still further to an abandonment and trust that all things will work together for good if we love God. Finally, this gives way to a joyful and generous giving. This is the giving that does not count the cost or heed the wounds, but simply gives lovingly and generously to others as we know God has given lovingly and generously to us. Isn't God still generous to us in his goodness, even when we have offended him? So we must love one another as he loved us.

Three Final Points

There are three final things to keep in mind. One of them is the prudence needed to bear wrongs patiently. Sometimes we are just not able to deal charitably with people who have offended us. We try our best to forgive them in our hearts, but we may have to avoid direct contact with them, especially if the harm was quite severe or recent. No matter how much we may want to forgive or be patient, contact with these people is likely to revive strong negative feelings within us. It may take awhile before we can inwardly settle our feelings of acceptance for someone who has hurt us deeply.

The second point to remember is that there are certain wrongs that should not be borne patiently but resisted or avoided. These are evils that affect people in an unjust way that will do harm to them. For example, if a wife is living in a physically abusive situation for herself or her children, she should not simply bear that patiently but do all that she needs to do to protect herself and/or her children from physical harm. Obviously, the same is true if someone, especially a minor, is being sexually abused. Another instance would be if one's good name is maligned unjustly. A person has a right to defend his good name and his well-being that may be adversely affected by slander, detraction or unjust actions. Sometimes one may need special guidance in these difficult situations.

The final thing we must always remember is that we cannot bear wrongs patiently without prayer. Only by asking the Lord for the grace to bear patiently with others, to accept the things that are difficult and to live with a certain amount of detachment and trust, can the needed transformation take place. We need the strength of Christ and the powerful working of the Holy Spirit to move from bitterness to sweetness. This is when we must recall the invitation of Jesus: "Come to me, all who labor and are heavy laden, and I will give you rest. Take my yoke upon you, and learn from me; for I am gentle and lowly in heart, and you will find rest for your souls. For my yoke is easy, and my burden is light" (Mt 11:28–30). Ultimately, it is only Jesus who can lighten the burden we must bear.

Forgive Offenses

The story is told of a prominent politician who was having a longstanding argument with a political opponent. The conflict became rather intense. Eventually, however, there was a breakthrough and the prominent politician succeeded in getting his way. At a later news conference, a reporter asked the politician, "Now you're going to forgive your opponent, aren't you, and make up with him?" The politician answered without hesitation, "Absolutely not! Forgiveness is a Christian thing, and I'm not a Christian!"

Jesus Practiced Mercy

The politician was right: forgiveness is a Christian thing! I believe we can say without doubt that forgiveness was one of the central themes of Jesus' life and teaching. He himself practiced it all through the three years of his public ministry. His greatest expression of forgiveness occurred when he prayed upon the Cross for those who were putting him to death: "Father, forgive them; for they know not what they do" (Lk 23:34).

All through his mission Jesus encountered occasions to exercise his great mercy, frequently by compassion for those in need but especially by forgiveness for repentant sinners. He forgave the penitent woman who wept over his feet.

Although she had many sins on her conscience, she turned to Jesus in profound sorrow for them. He acknowledged the great depth of her sincere love, forgave her and sent her away in peace (Lk 7:36–50). He also forgave the woman who was caught in adultery. He did not condone her sin: He told her not to sin again. But he who was without sin and could have thrown the first stone, taught us by his own example that God wills not condemnation, but mercy (Jn 8:3–11).

He also received those whose lives were in need of conversion. In Luke we read of the time Jesus went to the house of a chief tax collector named Zacchaeus. Some who witnessed this were scandalized by our Lord's behavior. They were shocked that Jesus had gone to stay in the home of a "public sinner", such as a tax collector. But Zacchaeus was a notorious sinner no longer: Jesus' kindness and mercy toward him brought the man to a profound conversion. He declared that for any act of injustice he had ever done to anyone he would repay that person four times as much as he took from them. He announced he would give half of his great wealth to the poor. Jesus' forgiveness had brought salvation to Zacchaeus and his household (Lk 19:1–10).

How different from the Pharisees was the attitude of Jesus. The Pharisees criticized our Lord for going to the house of Matthew whom he had just called to be an apostle. While enjoying a banquet with tax collectors and other "sinners" (all of whom the Pharisees condemned as non-observers of the law), Jesus set before the self-righteous Pharisees the challenge of mercy: "Those who are well have no need of a physician, but those who are sick. Go and learn what this means, 'I desire mercy, and not sacrifice.' For I came not to call the righteous, but sinners" (Mt 9:12–13).

Jesus Taught Mercy

It could be said that the theme of mercy was the center-piece of Jesus' moral teaching, because mercy unlocks the very heart of God himself! This was something taught by Jesus without any ambiguity, "Forgive, and you will be forgiven" (Lk 6:37). Our Lord had much to say about our need to forgive. In fact, he taught the message of mercy to us constantly in his preaching. Let us focus on three aspects of Jesus' teaching about mercy.

The Measure by Which We Forgive

Jesus tells us that he will deal with us in the same way and according to the same measure with which we deal with one another. We can sum it up by saying: What we give to others is what we ourselves will receive from the Lord. Jesus emphasizes this point about the measure of mercy:

> "Judge not, and you will not be judged; condemn not, and you will not be condemned; forgive, and you will be forgiven; give, and it will be given to you; good measure, pressed down, shaken together, running over, will be put into your lap. For the measure you give will be the measure you get back." (Lk 6:37–38)

We all carry the burden of our sins, the wrongs we do to offend God and to hurt one another. Therefore we always stand in need of God's mercy. We would be spiritually blind if we never acknowledged ourselves as sinners in need of forgiveness from God as well as from those whom we have offended. On the other hand, if we want God's forgiveness, we know we must be ready to forgive. This is what Jesus taught us to ask of our Heavenly Father in the prayer we call the Lord's Prayer: "forgive us our trespasses as we forgive those who trespass against us." Sometimes we may recite these words mechanically, without any thought to what we are really saying. But if we ever stop to realize what we are truly asking of God, then we would recognize how much we really need to forgive in order to be forgiven. A spiritual writer once said the most dangerous thing we could ever do is pray, because God may just take us at our word. He gave the example that if we were to ask God to change us, he may not leave us until he has broken every bone in our bodies to put us back together the way we should be! When it comes to asking for forgiveness, we had better first make sure that we have been forgiving others whatever injuries they have done to us. If we haven't been willing to forgive others, then asking God for forgiveness would not be exactly the prayer we would want to offer: he may just take us at our word!

This was the powerful point our Lord made in the parable about the ungrateful and merciless royal official (Mt 18:23–35). This parable is preceded by a question about forgiveness. "Then Peter . . . said to [Jesus]: 'Lord, how often shall my brother sin against me, and I forgive him? As many as seven times?' Jesus said to him, 'I do not say to you seven times, but seventy times seven'" (Mt 18:21–22). There is a very important point here. The Pharisees taught that a person only had to forgive three times. Peter probably thought he was being very generous because he was willing to forgive seven times. No doubt our Lord's words must have been a shock to him because Jesus said you had to multiply seven times by seventy. Our Lord did not literally mean that Peter had to forgive only 490 times. "Seven times seventy" was a Jewish expression that meant *as often as needed*. Jesus' teaching meant that even if we had already forgiven a number of injuries done to us by a certain individual, we would still have to forgive him should he injure us again. After all, God has forgiven us all our many past sins when we have asked him, and yet wouldn't he be ready to forgive our present and future sins if we asked again? Even if it were seven times seventy more sins?

The parable Jesus uses to illustrate this point is a comparison between two servants who owed debts. The first servant owed the king a debt that was so great that we might compare it to an individual owing the national debt of a country like the United States of America. Not even the richest person in America could make a dent in that debt. It was an unpayable amount. When the servant pleaded with the king for time to raise the money to pay what he owed, the king was so merciful that he actually wrote off the entire debt. There was a second servant who owed a debt to the first servant. His debt was a tiny fraction of the amount of the first debt It was actually payable, but the second servant needed time to raise the money. The first servant, who had been forgiven, would not hear of it. Following the custom of the day, he had the second servant along with his wife, children, and property sold into slavery to pay the smaller debt. When the king who had so generously forgiven the entire enormous debt of the first servant got word that this man had treated a fellow servant so mercilessly, the king was enraged and had the first servant with his family and possessions sold into slavery to pay a debt that was actually impossible to pay.

The point of the parable is that our sins against God take on a kind of infinite quality because it is God who is offended. There is no way that we can, of ourselves, make up for even one of our sins. But the offense of the second person was quite minor by comparison because the one offended did not have an infinite dignity as God has. So when someone offends us, we should be ready to forgive him in view of the great mercy God has in forgiving our injuries against him. Referring to the punishment the first servant received for refusing to forgive as he was forgiven, Jesus ends this parable by saying: "So also my heavenly Father will do to every one of you, if you do not forgive your brother from your heart" (Mt 18:35).

Mercy Opens the Heart of God

Our Lord stresses that it is important that we forgive our erring brothers and sisters from our hearts. If our prayer is to be heard, we must pray with a heart that is not closed or hardened by a lack of mercy. Otherwise, we will experience the heart of God closed to us when we offer our prayers and petitions to him. Jesus teaches us:

> So if you are offering your gift at the altar and there remember that your brother has something against you, leave your gift there before the altar and go; first be reconciled to your brother, and then come and offer your gift. (Mt 5:23–24)

Among the lives of the saints we find a moving example of someone who showed extraordinary mercy to another who had done him great harm, and how that mercy brought about a remarkable conversion. A Florentine nobleman named John had a brother who was murdered. According to a common practice of the day, he felt obligated to avenge his brother's death. With the help of some hired henchmen, he tracked down his brother's murderer. The man was unarmed, and John was about to slay him. It was Good Friday. As John approached, the man begged John to forgive him for killing his brother just as Jesus, on the first Good Friday, forgave those who were putting him to death on the Cross. At that moment John was deeply moved by God's grace. Throwing down his sword, he forgave the man who killed his brother and even embraced him. On his way home, he entered a Benedictine Church to pray, and the figure of Christ on the crucifix bowed his head to him in recognition of his generous act of mercy. Because he forgave so profoundly from his heart, John, the would-be murderer, received the grace to become a saint. He is known in Church history as Saint John Gaulbert. He died in 1073 and was canonized in 1193.

Forgive Even Your Enemies

Probably the most challenging form of mercy to practice is our Lord's command to forgive even our enemies. He taught this in the Sermon on the Mount. He began by quoting the Old Testament norm of moral behavior, "You shall love your neighbor and hate your enemy." What Jesus would teach us would be far different:

> "Love your enemies and pray for those who persecute you, so that you may be sons of your Father who is in heaven; for he makes his sun rise on the evil and on the good, and sends rain on the just and on the unjust. For if you love those who love you, what reward have you? Do not even the tax collectors do the same? And if you salute only your brethren, what more are you doing than others? Do not even the Gentiles do the same? You, therefore, must be perfect, as your heavenly Father is perfect." (Mt 5:44–48)

Our enemies include all who have done harm to us. We must forgive them because we wish to be forgiven. We have already seen an example of this in the story of the forgiveness of Saint John Gaulbert. What our Lord meant by "enemy", however, is not strictly someone who is out to kill us or someone we love. What Jesus meant by "enemy" also includes someone difficult to love, or toward whom we feel a certain repugnance, or whom we may even judge as unworthy of our love or kindness. In other words, an enemy can simply be a stranger whom we may never see again, someone who will not be able to do us good in return for anything good we may do for him. But we must still reach out with kindness and compassion if that brother or sister is in need, no matter who they are. The term "enemy" can also apply to notorious sinners like the woman caught in adultery; we do not condone the sinner's actions but we grant forgiveness because God loves the sinner and seeks to save him from his sins. Forgiving others for wrongs they may have done can give them the courage and trust to believe that even God would be ready to forgive them.

Jesus' teaching tells us that our love must be a love that costs us something to give. He contrasts this with the love that even pagans are capable of. For example, to love people who are friendly or kind to us does not require much effort. It comes naturally. To love someone who has hurt us is another story. But don't we want God to love us even after we have offended him by our sins? If we share only with those who would share with us, we are not doing any more than thieves would do. Rather, the love we give to our enemies, which has to be a very generous, giving love, makes us like our Heavenly Father. He sends the sunshine not only to good people but even to those who are bad! He lets the rain fall on the fields of the just and on the unjust as well. It is no surprise then that Saint Ignatius Loyola, founder of the Jesuits, is quoted as saying: "If you don't have an enemy, you had better go out and find one because you need an enemy to teach you how to love." This is because loving an enemy requires that we open our hearts more fully in order to forgive. Loving an enemy separates a convenient love from a sacrificial, total, and self-forgetting love.

Why Do We Not Forgive?

Alexander Pope has expressed so well the meaning of mercy when he said: "To err is human; to forgive divine." Mercy is considered the most characteristic attribute of God himself. As we pray twenty-six times in Psalm 136, "for his mercy endures for ever". If we ourselves many times fail to forgive as we should, we need humbly to remember: "to err is human". Sometimes we contradict ourselves so obviously in this matter. It was said that outside of a religious house there was a sign: "Private Property! No trespassing! Violators will be prosecuted to the fullest extent of the law!" It was signed "Religious of Divine Mercy".

If forgiveness is so important, both to receive for the wrongs we have done as well as to give to others who have injured us, we must ask: "Why do we not forgive?" Here are some reasons that may hinder us from forgiving.

Extreme Sensitiveness

If we are ultra-sensitive to things that people may say about us or do to us, we can easily exaggerate the hurts that we suffer. A slight injury may be blown out of proportion and become a great offense, or some injury that is more imagined than real can turn us with a hard heart against someone. Sometimes extreme sensitivity can make us deal with hurts in very bizarre ways. A story was told about a woman who apparently was very sensitive. She wrote a number of letters that she called her "after letters". In these letters she wrote to people she felt had hurt her by their words or deeds or thoughtlessness. She was going to put it in her will that after she died these letters would be mailed out to all the people she felt had offended her. In this way they would feel upset that they hurt this poor lady and now that she was gone there was no opportunity to express their apologies or seek reconciliation. If we want to find mercy, it would be wise to deal with things that we find offensive as soon as possible. This way they will not be exaggerated in our minds and hearts.

Living in the Past

Somewhat like people who are extremely sensitive are people who brood over past hurts. In this way they keep those old hurts very fresh and alive in their hearts. When they speak about injuries that occurred twenty-five years ago, they make it sound as if they happened twenty-five minutes ago! People who always bring up the past in their arguments need to stop living in the past. How can they do that? First of all, make an effort to resolve past injuries by forgiving from the heart. Let these things go. How many families have brothers and sisters, or parents and children, who have remained divided for years and years because of things that happened when they were young. Walls of silence were built up because they couldn't let go of the past!

Another thing to avoid is replaying the "old tapes" in our minds, reviewing over and over again all the injustices and hurts that others have done to us. That is a formula for bitterness and unhappiness. We all need to make our peace with the past, and forgiveness is a very important part of that process. Once we have made peace, accepting what has happened or forgiving those who have actually injured us, then we can let go of the past, live in the present and hope for the future with joy and happiness. The last thing we want to happen is to grow old being bitter over negative experiences in the past. Some of the best advice I ever came across was the saying "Remember the best; forget the rest." That is a formula for peace and happiness in the heart and the family.

Pride

Many people refuse to forgive because of a false sense of pride. They feel that their honor has been offended and so they refuse to let go of the injury that was done to them. As recently as nineteenth-century America, people would even resort to a duel to the death as revenge for the injury done to their honor. The Church has always condemned duels because it results in both a homicide and suicide. No one has the right to take the life of another nor do they have the right to expose their own life to an untimely death. The Christian way to resolve differences is to grant forgiveness. A story is told about a priest who was preaching a parish mission in New York City. During the mission, a woman came to ask the priest to come to her home and hear the confession of her husband who was confined to bed. Before the priest entered the room of the husband, the wife told the priest that her husband had not been to confession for many years. She said the reason was that he would not forgive someone who had offended him years before. She pleaded with the priest: "Please get my husband to forgive!" When the priest entered the man's room, he asked the man if he wanted to go to confession. The man said "all right". Then the priest addressed the need to forgive. "Your wife told me that there was someone who injured you whom you have not forgiven. Don't you realize that if you want God to forgive you your sins, you must forgive others in any ways they have offended you?" The man responded angrily, "If the only way God would forgive me my sins is for me to forgive the injury done to me by this person, I would rather burn in Hell for all eternity before forgiving him." Sometimes the hardness of anger can make us so blind to the obvious. Imagine, someone willing to risk the punishment of Hell for all eternity because of some offense done here on earth. We can only hope and pray that the man had a change of heart and forgave his enemy before he died.

Vengeance

Vengeance, or the desire to get back at someone who has offended us, often follows from a false sense of pride. This desire to inflict hurt on someone who has hurt us easily arises in a heart that is filled with bitterness. One needs to learn to let go. Saint Paul gives this very important teaching to the ancient Romans in his letter to them:

> Repay no one evil for evil, but take thought for what is noble in the sight of all. If possible, so far as it depends upon you, live peaceably with all. Beloved, never avenge yourselves, but leave it to the wrath of God; for it is written, "Vengeance is mine, I will repay, says the Lord." No, "if your enemy is hungry, feed him; if he is thirsty, give him drink . . ." Do not be overcome by evil, but overcome evil with good. (Rom 12:17–21)

Mercy Brings the Beauty of New Life

Mercy can transform a person's life, as we saw in the example of Saint John Gaulbert. Letting go of hurts, especially those that are longstanding, sets the heart free to receive God's grace and peace. This applies not only to the one who forgives but even to the one who is forgiven. Saint Augustine said that it was Saint Stephen's prayer to forgive those who were stoning him to death, "Lord, do not hold this sin against them" (Acts 7:60), that won the grace of conversion for Saul of Tarsus to become the great Apostle Saint Paul. It was also the prayer of the dying Saint Maria Goretti, "Lord, forgive Alexander" that ultimately won the grace of conversion for her murderer Alexander Serenelli from a life of sin to one of sanctity.

Our Lord shows the beauty of the effects of mercy in his parables of mercy (Lk 15:1–32). In the parables of the lost sheep and the lost coin, the Lord tells us how he seeks sinners with such great compassion, like a shepherd leaving ninety-nine other sheep in a deserted area simply to find one that was lost, or like a woman who nearly turns her house upside down to find one missing coin. In the same way, the Lord rejoices to bring back those who have strayed. Mercy finds them! Finally, in the deeply touching story of the prodigal son, we see God's attitude reflected in the father who must have looked down the road every day hoping and expecting that his wayward son would return. When he did, a great celebration began. Jesus assures us that there is likewise more joy in Heaven over one sinner who repents than over ninety-nine who do not need to repent. The same can be said of those who forgive, that there is more joy in Heaven over one who forgives his brother or sister from his heart than over ninety-nine who do not need to forgive.

Comfort the Sorrowful

A popular story in the Eastern Church vividly illustrates the spiritual work of mercy of comforting the sorrowful. It was said that when the apostle Saint Andrew died and arrived at the gates of Heaven, his brother, Saint Peter, was already on the job as gatekeeper. When Andrew saw his brother he asked, "Peter, where is she?" Peter knew exactly who "she" was: our Blessed Lady. Peter replied to his brother, "Andrew, she is not up here. She is down on earth drying the eyes of her children in the 'valley of tears'". How often our Blessed Lady must come down from Heaven to comfort her sorrowful children.

Sorrow and suffering are unavoidable aspects of life. They are the result of sin, both Original Sin and our personal sins. They come to everyone: the good and the bad, the saints and the sinners. Even our joys are mixed with sorrows. Archbishop Sheen used to say, "There is no Easter Sunday without a Good Friday." Or as an old Italian proverb puts it, "There is no rose without its thorns."

Jesus, our Blessed Savior, experienced both joy and sorrow in his lifetime. So did his holy Mother, since she shared fully in his joys and sorrows. At the Last Supper, Jesus talked about both joy and sorrow to his disciples. He assured them, however, that ultimately joy will endure, joy will win out. "As the Father has loved me, so have I loved you; abide in my love. If you keep my commandments, you will abide

in my love, just as I have kept my Father's commandments
and abide in his love. These things I have spoken to you,
that my joy may be in you, and that your joy may be full"
(Jn 15:9–11). Jesus stressed the fact that we are called to
share his joy. How the disciples must have rejoiced to hear
this message. But almost immediately, our Lord spoke of
a profound sorrow which his apostles would also experience: "Truly, truly, I say to you, you will weep and lament,
but the world will rejoice; you will be sorrowful, but your
sorrow will turn into joy" (Jn 16:20). The apostles would
not be spared the cross, for no disciple is greater than his
master. If Jesus suffered, then his closest companions would
also suffer (Jn 15:20). But what is remarkable in our Lord's
statement about suffering is his assertion that our very grief
and sorrow would become the "raw materials", so to speak,
from which our joy would come. He illustrated this with
a wonderful example: "When a woman is in labor, she has
pain, because her hour has come; but when she is delivered
of the child, she no longer remembers the anguish, for joy
that a child is born into the world. So you have sorrow now,
but I will see you again and your hearts will rejoice, and
no one will take your joy from you" (Jn 16:21–22). As
a mother's pain in childbearing is transformed into joy by
holding her newborn infant, so our sufferings in this vale
of tears will be transformed into a joyous love of God, both
in this world and in the next.

Causes, Effects, and Remedies

Not all sorrow is the same because it has different causes. As
a result, not all sorrow can be comforted in the same way.

Destructive Sorrow

Some forms of sorrow are bad because they result from a distorted self-centered love. These are healed by removing the negative roots that give rise to such sorrow. For example, there is "worldly sorrow", which is the sorrow that results from material losses, whether money, popularity, possessions or even social status. For a Christian, the remedy for such a sorrow is to remember that our real treasures are not those we accumulate here on earth but those that await us in the Kingdom of Heaven. Jesus himself had said, "What does it profit a man, to gain the whole world and forfeit his life?" (Mk 8:36). Elsewhere Jesus said, "No servant can serve two masters; for either he will hate the one and love the other, or he will be devoted to the one and despise the other. You cannot serve God and mammon" (Lk 16:13). When the desire and the hope for "heavenly treasure" begins, "worldly sorrow" will end.

Another negative form of sorrow is despair, which is sorrow without hope. The person who gives in to despair feels that all his bridges have been burnt behind him and there is never a way to go back. This is the sorrow Judas experienced when he realized he had betrayed the Lord with a kiss. It led him to take his own life because he believed the Lord could never forgive him. The antidote to despair is God's mercy, which is greater than any evil we could ever do. In our sorrows, let us remember the words of Saint Paul to "not grieve as others do who have no hope" (1 Thess 4:13).

A final form of negative sorrow is self-pity. Self-pity results from an exaggerated focus on all our trials, sufferings, and problems. This frequently stems from the narcissistic or self-centered view of life so prevalent in modern society. It is often based on an underlying, unspoken principle: "Life should always make me happy, and when I am not, I am getting cheated." Narcissistic people need to break out of the imprisonment of self-pity. Nothing will make a person so miserable in life as always looking only at the difficulties they must endure. We need a balanced picture. As the old saying goes, "I complained I had no shoes until I met a man who had no feet." We all have blessings that we must recognize and be grateful for. They are really gifts of God. When we recognize and embrace them as such, we will begin to experience joy in life. This true joy is the real antidote to the sorrow of self-pity!

Beneficial Sorrow

Other forms of sorrow can be good and even the source of great consolation. One such sorrow is sorrow for one's own sins. This can lead us to confess our sins and seek God's forgiveness. This was the sorrow of Saint Peter, who after denying the Lord three times went out and wept bitterly (Lk 22:62). It is said his sorrow was renewed every time he heard a rooster crow. Even at his hour of death, he never forgot his sorrow, for he asked his executioners to crucify him upside down because he was not worthy to die like his master! This kind of sorrow often brings peace of mind and heart and the beginning of a new life.

Another form of sorrow that brings many blessings is the sorrow for the sins of others. It is one thing to offer prayers and tears for our own sins. But it can be even more fruitful when we sorrow for the conversion of sinners. Saint Monica shed many tears for the conversion of her wayward son who later became the great Saint Augustine. During her sixteen long years of praying for the conversion of her son, she would go twice a day, morning and evening, to pray in the church for his conversion. It was said that wherever she knelt in prayer, the floor became wet from her many tears. A bishop once consoled her with the remark, "It is impossible that the son of so many tears could ever be lost." Monica's tears only ended when Augustine's tears began!

A third beneficial sorrow is the sorrow of compassion, which leads us to comfort others in their need and suffering. This was the compassion that Jesus spontaneously showed the widow of Nain who had lost her only son (Lk 7:12–15). We see his compassion again in the raising of his good friend Lazarus from the dead, thus comforting Lazarus' sisters Martha and Mary, all of whom Jesus loved deeply (Jn 11:1–44.).

We All Need Consolation

God Provides Consolation

In the midst of life's sorrows, we all need to be comforted, and sometimes God himself provides the necessary consolation. Jesus experienced consolation from his Heavenly Father. After fasting for forty days and then being tempted by the devil, "behold, angels came and ministered to him" (Mt 4:11). During his agony in the garden, when he sorrowed "even to death" (Mt 26:38) and suffered so intensely that his sweat became like drops of blood, an angel from Heaven came to strengthen him (Lk 22:43).

In our own lives, we can experience a direct consolation from God. Sometimes he guides us, other times he strengthens us, and still other times he comforts us. For example,

God gives the gift of interior peace to many who are troubled. He also grants the comfort of forgiveness when we fall into sin and repent. The apostles, for example, experienced this consolation in their suffering for Christ. After they had been strengthened by receiving the Holy Spirit at Pentecost, they were later scourged by order of the Sanhedrin. What was their reaction? "Then they left the presence of the council, rejoicing that they were counted worthy to suffer dishonor for the name" (Acts 5:41). These were the same apostles who had fled from Jesus in panic and fear for their lives on Holy Thursday night! Their sorrow and distress was turned into joy by the power of the Holy Spirit.

Another example is found in the lives of the three young visionaries of Fatima: Lucia, Francesco, and Jacinta. Our Lady herself promised to be their comfort in the midst of the trials that they were willing to accept from God as part of his plan for the salvation of the world. They courageously and generously agreed to do God's will. They were not spared sorrow, but when our Lady came to comfort them, their sorrow was turned into joy.

Comfort Comes through Others

Though God can comfort us directly in our minds and hearts, we all experience times when we need the consolation of other human beings. When one member of a family is in difficulty or suffering, family members gather around to support and bring comfort. A spiritual director can ease the fears and doubts that often assail us on our spiritual journey. A brother or sister in Christ can be God's instrument to reassure a little one troubled by daily problems. In other words, we all need a comfort at times that is more tangible and concrete.

We can say that in these situations God sends his "earthly angels" to console us. Here are some instances I am sure we have all experienced. When a person is disturbed by fears about their future or their ability to accomplish the tasks that face them, they can try to encourage themselves by "positive thinking". This can be important and helpful to a certain extent. However, if we hear someone else, particularly someone we look up to or believe to be especially competent, tell us there is nothing to fear, our fears evaporate more quickly and more completely. Another example occurs when we are trying to make sense of things that are distressing us. We need answers to our questions, especially those that begin with "Why?" or "Why me?" Often we are too close to the situation to see it clearly. But someone outside us can often grasp the whole picture in ways that we cannot. Their perspective, wisdom, and reassurance can do wonders to calm us. Another comfort we draw from others is just being able to unburden our cares and worries to a listening heart. It can be a great relief to our minds that someone else knows and understands some of the personal trials and difficulties we are going through, things we cannot share with everyone. That listening person becomes like an "angel" ministering to us.

The Comfort of Forgiveness

One of the most important forms of comfort we can receive through others is in the sacrament of reconciliation. For some sins a person may make a thousand acts of contrition and yet never feel these sins have been forgiven. What a remarkable effect, however, are the words of absolution by a priest in confession to persons who have just unburdened themselves of their deepest and most distressing

secrets. When our Lord established confession as a sacrament, he knew we needed to speak our sins to another and
hear those definitive words pronounced over us: "I absolve
you from your sins, in the name of the Father, and of the
Son, and of the Holy Spirit." How incredibly reassuring!

Ways to Comfort the Sorrowful

We have many opportunities to comfort the sorrowful. The
person experiencing sorrow may be a relative, a parishioner,
a neighbor, or someone in a nursing home or hospice care.
Sometimes we can bring comfort just by offering a listening ear and a compassionate heart. People in their sorrow
often need to talk, and that requires someone to be there to
listen. I remember a woman who came to me with family
concerns and talked for nearly an hour straight. She ended
by saying, "Thank you, Father, for helping me so much!"
I did nothing but listen.

If we hear someone is sick, a greeting card or a little note
offering assurance of our prayers would be a comfort. Providing a person with an inspiring book to read or a helpful recording can bring peace of mind and heart. Going to
visit someone who is sick, calling a distant friend, sending
a sympathy card at the time of the loss of a loved one are all
forms of comfort. Even going shopping for someone who
is distraught or preparing a meal to bring to the home of
such a person is a great help.

There may be cases where professional help, such as a
doctor, psychologist, or a health aide may be needed. We
may be able to encourage people to seek the type of professional assistance they need. This often happens in cases of the
elderly who can no longer live alone but may be frightened

or disturbed at the prospect of leaving their home for an assisted living or a nursing home environment. The advice of a friend can be a great comfort in such circumstances.

We Can Comfort but Not Necessarily Heal

There is one final point we should keep very much in mind. Many people are discouraged from reaching out to comfort others in their sorrow, especially at the loss of a loved one or in the case of a serious accident. They feel awkward because they see someone in pain and yet are keenly aware that they cannot remove the source of the pain. Remember, any attempt to comfort in these situations does not mean we can take the sorrow away. We are not called to perform the miracles of Jesus, who raised the dead and healed the sick. But we can be there to express our compassion and to share in their sorrow. We can pray with them that they may find the comfort and strength to bear up in their pain.

Only God can remove every sorrow. Usually it is time itself that he uses to heal suffering. But we can be his instruments to help one another here and now. We can do this through small acts of kindness, hope, and joy. Sometimes the remedy can be so simple. As Mother Teresa of Calcutta often said, "The road to peace begins with a smile."

Pray for the Living and the Dead

"Father, say a prayer for me!" "Sister, please pray for me!" Probably every Catholic priest and religious has heard these words countless times. Sometimes people just make a general prayer request. At other times, they have very specific intentions. Whatever the need, people are sure to ask for prayers of petition because they are convinced of their power. After all, our Lord assures us: "Ask, and it will be given you; seek, and you will find; knock, and it will be opened to you. For every one who asks receives, and he who seeks finds, and to him who knocks it will be opened" (Lk 11:9-10). This is especially true of the power of intercessory prayer.

Jesus and Mary Intercede for Us

Jesus the High Priest

In his humanity, Jesus is our high priest before the Father. This means that he is a mediator between the Father and all of mankind. His role is to intercede for us in prayer. He presents our needs to the Father and pleads for mercy for our sins. No doubt the most outstanding example of Jesus interceding for the Father's mercy came when he prayed on the Cross, "Father, forgive them; for they know not what they do" (Lk 23:34). He pleaded for mercy, not only for those who were actually carrying out his crucifixion, but also for all of us for whom he was dying to take away our sins. Our sins were the real cause of his death. We must imitate this example of our Lord and be ready to pray for others, even those who cause us difficulties or who may even wish to harm us. This would fulfill what our Lord himself taught us not only by his example here, but also by his words. In the Sermon on the Mount he told us:

> You have heard that it was said, "You shall love your neighbor and hate your enemy." But I say to you, Love your enemies, and pray for those who persecute you, that you may be sons of your Father who is in Heaven; for he makes his sun rise on the evil and on the good, and sends rain on the just and on the unjust. (Mt 5:43–45)

Another powerful example of Jesus' intercessory prayer is found in the Last Supper account. Jesus turned to Peter whom he had made the leader among the apostles, and said to him, "Simon, Simon, behold, Satan demanded to have you, that he might sift you like wheat, but I have prayed for you that your faith may not fail; and when you have turned again, strengthen your brethren" (Lk 22:31–32). The Lord prayed for strength for Peter both for himself and for the other apostles. Do we imitate Jesus' prayer by praying for others in their special needs? We may learn of someone going through a trial; through our prayers we can support them to have courage and go on. We may learn of someone who is tempted to give up his faith or to fall into a sinful situation. In the face of the weakness of the flesh, our prayers can be a source of moral strength for others. If our love is to grow, it is necessary to expand the focus of our prayers to include the concerns we have for those who are in trial and tribulation.

Mary, Our Mother

Our Lady was no doubt the closest imitator of Jesus. Just as he prayed for others, we find evidence of Mary bringing the needs of others to her Divine Son. For example, at the wedding feast of Cana, our Lady makes known to Jesus the need of the young couple whose celebration they were attending. Her prayer of concern was simple yet powerful, "They have no wine" (Jn 2:3). Our Lady's concern was for the young couple not to be embarrassed by a lack of wine for their guests. This probably would have forced them to cut short their weeklong wedding celebration. She was not asked to do something; she spontaneously saw the need and offered her words of intercession. They were very powerful because they moved Jesus to work his first miracle. And this happened despite the fact that he had indicated that it was not the time for him to reveal himself: "My hour has not yet come" (Jn 2:4). Because of this miracle Jesus worked at her request, he "manifested his glory; and his disciples believed in him" (Jn 2:11). The marvel of Jesus' first miracle was the result of a humble but trusting plea of intercession by his mother. In our own lives, let us imitate Mary's spirit of spontaneously interceding for those who are in genuine need.

We see our Lady again in an intercessory role springing from her spiritual motherhood of the Church. For nine days prior to the great feast of Pentecost, she was surrounded by the apostles and the first band of Jesus' disciples gathered together in the Upper Room in Jerusalem. They were prayerfully awaiting the promised gift of the Holy Spirit: "All these with one accord devoted themselves to prayer, together with the women and Mary the mother of Jesus, and with his brethren" (Acts 1:14). Mary is joining her prayers to those of the first members of the Church, praying for the gift of the Holy Spirit to come. How powerful her intercession must have been, to move the Holy Spirit to come! After all, he had already come upon her at Nazareth. At the precise moment she was overshadowed by the Holy Spirit, the Second Divine Person of the Blessed Trinity became man in her womb. Pope John Paul II called this the greatest event in human history. At Pentecost another great event would take place: Namely, the Church was born when the Spirit came. Our prayers of intercession imitate the example Mary gives us in praying for the needs of our brothers and sisters in Christ. In a special way we should pray often for the many needs of the Church in our times. Do we pray for vocations? Or for our brothers and sisters in Christ who are persecuted? Or for the message of the gospel to be spread by zealous missionaries in our time?

Other Examples of Intercession in Sacred Scripture

Old Testament

In the Old Testament Book of Exodus we have a powerful example of Moses intervening to save the Jewish people from God's just wrath. The people had worshipped a pagan image of a golden calf and even sacrificed to it, and God threatened to punish them.

> But Moses begged the LORD his God, and said, "O LORD, why does your wrath burn hot against your people, whom you have brought forth out of the land of Egypt with great

power and with a mighty hand?" . . . And the LORD repented
of the evil which he thought to do to his people. (Ex 32:9–
11, 14)

When we pray for peace in the world, ultimately we are praying that God will not punish us for our sins just as Moses
implored God's mercy when his people had worshipped a
false god. We should always pray that God will forgive us
our own sins as well as the sins of our brothers.

Another dramatic Old Testament example of intercession
involves the great prophet Elijah. He had stayed with a
widow in Zarephath who took care of his needs for food
and drink for a whole year during a famine. Her son became severely sick and died. The prophet interceded on behalf of the child's life praying: "'O LORD my God, let this
child's soul come into him again.' And the LORD listened to
the voice of Elijah; and the soul of the child came into him
again, and he revived" (1 Kings 17:21–22). Elijah's prayer
was powerful because it was the prayer of a very holy man.
He prayed intensely for the sake of the woman who had
showed him such kindness. When our prayers of intercession are motivated by compassion for those whom we see
suffering, they take on a special strength because they are
pleasing to God.

New Testament

In the New Testament we also see evidence of the power of
intercessory prayer. Saint Paul was one who believed in its
power. He himself prayed often for his converts. He begins
his letter to the Philippians with a beautiful sentiment of a
prayer of thanksgiving. He writes:

> I thank my God in all my remembrance of you, always in
> every prayer of mine for you all making my prayer with joy,

thankful for your partnership in the gospel from the first
day until now. . . . And it is my prayer that your love may
abound more and more, with knowledge and all discernment, so that you may approve what is excellent, and may
be pure and blameless for the day of Christ, filled with the
fruits of righteousness which come through Jesus Christ, to
the glory and praise of God (Phil 1:3–5, 9–11).

The great Apostle of the Gentiles held close to his heart
all his converts in the various churches he established and
remembered them continuously in prayer.

Saint Paul not only prayed for others, but he sought their
prayers as well. He ends his letter to the Ephesians with this
beautiful plea for prayer for himself as well as all those who
are promoting the gospel:

Pray at all times in the Spirit, with all prayer and supplication. To that end keep alert with all perseverance, making
supplication for all the saints and also for me, that utterance
may be given me in opening my mouth boldly to proclaim
the mystery of the gospel, for which I am an ambassador
in chains; that I may declare it boldly, as I ought to speak.
(Eph 6:18–20)

The Early Church

We have already seen a great example of the power of common prayer in the early Church. We read in the book of Acts
that King Herod began to persecute the church (12:1ff.).
He martyred Saint James and went on to arrest Peter. "And
when he had seized [Peter] he put him in prison, and delivered him to four squads of soldiers to guard him, intending
after the Passover to bring him out to the people. So Peter
was kept in prison; but earnest prayer for him was made to
God by the Church" (vv. 4–5). As a result of this common

prayer, Peter was miraculously freed from the prison by the intervention of an angel. When he arrived at the place where the Christian community was assembled, "he went to the house of Mary, the mother of John whose other name was Mark, where many were gathered together and were praying" (v. 12). Our Lord himself told how powerful this kind of prayer could be. "Again I say to you, if two of you agree on earth about anything they ask, it will be done for them by my Father in heaven. For where two or three are gathered in my name, there am I in the midst of them" (Mt 18:19-20). We experience this power of communal prayer today when we pray together with other Christians at a prayer meeting, or say the family rosary, or are joined in prayer for common petition.

The Saints Are Always Interceding for Us

Saint Padre Pio

It is no surprise that saintly people like Padre Pio were constantly sought after for their prayers. A few days before he died, this great Franciscan mystic of the twentieth century was asked by his religious superior, "What do you want written on your tombstone?" The Saint answered: "Write down: 'Here lies a priest who prayed.'" And pray he did. We could say of him what was said of Saint Francis of Assisi: "He was not so much a man of prayer as he had become prayer personified." Padre Pio spent two hours each morning in preparation for his daily Mass, which itself sometimes lasted longer than two hours. In addition he always made a fifteen-minute thanksgiving after Holy Communion at the end of Mass. He also prayed the Rosary constantly throughout the day.

The reason Padre Pio's Masses were long was because he interceded for numerous people, both living and dead. He always prayed the Roman Canon at Mass which was the only Eucharistic prayer used during his lifetime. Before the Consecration there is a place to remember the living, and after the Consecration there is a similar place to remember the dead. Padre Pio would spend at each of those two places of prayer as much as twenty-five minutes. He had many of the living to pray for. For example, he prayed for his penitents. Hearing confessions on an average of fifteen hours a day, he heard as many as three hundred confessions daily. No doubt he prayed in general for all of them but he may have remembered specific persons with a longer prayer. He also prayed for those he called his "spiritual children" to whom he gave spiritual direction and guidance. Some of them lived near his friary in southern Italy, while others were scattered throughout the world. No doubt he carried their needs before the Lord at Mass. It is also estimated that he received between eight and ten thousand letters a week from people who sought his guidance, his blessing, and his prayers. He would even tell people to "send me your guardian angel" if they had to bring urgent needs to him so he could pray for them. Sometimes he was approached with unusual requests for his prayers, like the lady who asked him to pray for her husband to find work. When the Padre asked what kind of work he did, she answered, "He's an undertaker"!

Saint Padre Pio also prayed for the dead. He had a great love for the souls in Purgatory. In his later years, after the building of a new church, there were over a thousand people at his Mass each day. He was once asked if any souls from Purgatory ever came to his Mass. He answered: "More people come to my Mass from Purgatory than do the living!" Stories abound that souls in Purgatory were allowed to appear to him and request his prayers. One such story involved a Capuchin novice who had been stationed at the friary about one hundred years before Padre Pio lived there. He appeared to the saint one night in the chapel. Padre Pio asked who he was. He answered: "I was a novice in this friary a hundred years ago. I did not do my work as sacristan! I am now in Purgatory doing my job. Please pray for me!" Padre Pio prayed for the novice and he never saw him again. Presumably he had gone to Heaven.

Saint Faustina Kowalska

We find another powerful testimony to the importance of praying for others in the diary of Saint Faustina Kowalska. It is an incident that involves her own sister.

> My sister [Wanda] came to see me today. When she told me of her plans, I was horror-stricken. How is such a thing possible? Such a beautiful little soul before the Lord, and yet, great darkness had come over her, and she did not know how to help herself. She had a dark view of everything. The good God entrusted her to my care, and for two weeks I was able to work with her. But how many sacrifices this soul cost me is known only to God. For no other soul did I bring so many sacrifices and sufferings and prayers before the throne of God as I did for her soul. I felt that I had forced God to grant her grace. When I reflect on all this, I see that it was truly a miracle. Now I can see how much power intercessory prayer has before God.[1]

The Power of Intercessory Prayer

Most Catholics and even devout members of other religions know and instinctively trust the power of prayer. As an old

[1] Maria Faustina Kowalska, *Divine Mercy in My Soul* (Stockbridge, Mass.: Marian Press, 2007), p. 107.

saying puts it, "There are more things wrought by the power of prayer than this world imagines!" And people who pray know this power. When we pray for others, whether living or deceased, we are praying the "prayer of intercession". We are asking God on behalf of others to bestow his graces, his providential care, his guidance, and his mercy. The intentions we need to pray for are almost endless.

We should pray for the needs of the Church. This means, first of all, to pray for our Holy Father, the Pope, because he carries enormous burdens as the Supreme Shepherd of our Church. We can only imagine the tremendous concerns he has for the needs of the Church throughout the world! We should also pray for our bishops, for their burden is not an easy one. They are often criticized for difficult and painful decisions they must make, such as to close a parish church that can no longer sustain itself. Archbishop Sheen once commented on Saint Paul's remark that it was a good thing to desire to be a bishop. He said the Apostle said this because he knew that in his day bishops were sure to be martyred. Archbishop Sheen added: "Today, the martyrdom of bishops comes in different ways." They need our prayers! We should also pray for our pastors and all the priests who minister to us as well as the religious women and men who work for our spiritual good. Jesus himself said we should pray for more religious and priestly vocations in the Church when he told us to ask our Heavenly Father, the Lord of the harvest, to send more laborers to gather in the harvest.

Then there are the needs of the world. First and foremost, we should pray for the end of the culture of death, namely the end of abortion, euthanasia, embryonic stem cell research, infanticide, and all those other attacks on the sanctity of life from conception to natural death. Furthermore, we pray for world peace, the end of wars, terrorism, and the like. We should pray for world leaders that they be guided by principles of justice and peace. Furthermore, we remember those who are victims of tragedies and poverty and all forms of human suffering.

Finally, we pray for the spiritual needs of people. Primary among them is the prayer for the conversion of sinners and especially for the dying, that God will grant the grace of a happy death and a merciful judgment. Like Saint Monica praying for the conversion of her son, Saint Augustine, we must often persevere in heartfelt prayer for the conversions of those we love. We can pray for the spread of Eucharistic devotion, for the work of evangelization, and for the renewal of Catholic piety, especially the renewal of the sacrament of confession, which has been neglected in our time.

Praying for Our Own Personal Needs

This does not mean that we should not pray for ourselves, because we all have our own physical as well as spiritual needs. Some people have the mistaken notion that they should not pray for themselves. This is a false idea. After all, Jesus taught us: "You shall love your neighbor as yourself" (Mt 22:39). If we pray for the needs of our neighbors because we love them, must we not pray also for our own needs because we have a proper love of ourselves? Jesus assumes that we have this proper love of ourselves in order to properly love our neighbor. It is a self-centered or distorted self-love that we must condemn and reject, not a love of self that is properly in line with God's love. Let us look at an example that Jesus himself gives us. When he gave his disciples the Lord's Prayer, he taught us petitions that are directed at our own personal needs: "Give us this day our daily bread"; "forgive us our trespasses . . ."; "lead us not into temptation . . .";

"deliver us from evil" (Mt 6:11–13). The saints assure us that we must pray to God daily for the graces needed for our salvation. One of the favorite sayings of many saints is "Pray as if it all depends on God; then go out and work as if it all depends on you."

Praying for Others

The spiritual work of mercy to pray for the living and the dead reminds us that we have a mission to pray for others. Since each one of us is a member of the Mystical Body of Christ, the Church, each of us has a responsibility to pray for the good of the whole Church as well as for those whose lives we personally touch. The idea of praying for the living and the dead is connected with the communion of saints, who are all united in the three-fold structure of the Church.

First there are the members of the Church who are still alive on earth. This aspect of the Mystical Body is called the "Church militant" because, as Saint Paul says, we are still fighting "the good fight" (2 Tim 4–7). This means we are still striving to resist the temptations of the world, the flesh, and the devil (pride) by practicing the Christian virtues. Not only do we ourselves need God's grace to do this, but so do our brothers and sisters in Christ. Many of them are not praying for themselves. And so we need to pray for them. Our Lady in her message at Fatima reminded us of this important point when she told the three little children, Lucia, Francesco, and Jacinta: "Many souls are lost from God because there is no one to pray and to offer sacrifices for them." Therefore, we must pray for them that they will receive from God all the graces they need to serve him faithfully and win the crown of eternal salvation.

The second aspect of the Mystical Body is called the

"Church suffering". These are the souls in Purgatory who are being purified through suffering from the last vestiges of sin. Once purified, they can enter Heaven where they will enjoy the beatific vision of God for all eternity. They will be among the saints in God's Kingdom. It is our understanding that the souls in Purgatory cannot pray for themselves but merely endure their purifying sufferings. It is we who can pray for them to assist them more quickly through their intense sufferings. This is one of the reasons why the Church has the practice of offering Masses for the repose of the souls of those who die. Many of them need the abundant merits of the Holy Sacrifice of the Mass to help them. The Church also has the special remembrance of the souls in Purgatory on November 2, All Souls' Day, as well as throughout the entire month of November. The greatest thing we can do for our loved ones who have died and for any of the souls in Purgatory is to pray that they will be quickly released to go to Heaven. Many people frequently offer prayers for "those souls in Purgatory who have no one to pray for them". No doubt they will pray for us if we are in a similar situation of need. If those we pray for are already in Heaven, God will certainly give the graces to another needy soul.

The third aspect of the Mystical Body is the "Church triumphant". These are the saints in Heaven who are enjoying the bliss of eternal life. We do not pray for them since they do not need our prayers any longer. They have reached their eternal goal and won their crowns in Heaven. But we pray *to* them because they greatly help us through their powerful intercession with almighty God. This belief is found in our Liturgy of the Eucharist. For example, Eucharistic Prayer III contains these beautiful words: "May he make us an everlasting gift to you and enable us to share in the inheritance of your saints, with Mary, the virgin Mother of

God, with the apostles, the martyrs, and all your saints, on whose constant intercession we rely for help."

We invoke the intercession of the saints to plead before God's heavenly throne for our needs and the needs of others. Some people feel that it is wrong to ask the prayers of the saints or even the prayers of the faithful on earth. They have the mistaken notion that we should always go "directly to God" and not through others. They would argue that God loves all of us, and so he will listen to each of us when we pray directly to him. This is true only to a certain extent. God does love us, but we also have our sins, and those he does not love. So the power of our prayers is limited. But the saints are very close to God and very pleasing to him for they no longer have sin in their lives. We can apply to the intercession of the saints what often applies in the business world: "It's not what you know but who you know." The saints can get right through where we may stumble. After all, they enjoy God's deepest love and friendship. The saints, in their great love for us, would desire nothing more than to assist us by their prayers so that someday those of us who are still on earth as well as the souls in Purgatory will be among their number praising God forever in Heaven.

Conclusion

Let Us Practice the Works of Mercy Every Day

We have looked at the corporal and spiritual works of mercy as they have come to us in sacred Scripture and the teachings of the Church. Now, our challenge is to live them each day. We should do this for three reasons.

1. To Live Our Christian Vocation and Fulfill the Mission of the Church

The love that we show to one another by living out the works of mercy is the sign of our true Christian vocation. We see this clearly in the Gospel where Jesus tells us that we will be known as his disciples by the love we have for one another (see Jn 13:35). When we carry out the works of mercy we fulfill Jesus' commandment to "love one another as I have loved you" (Jn 15:12) because the works of mercy are the very fruits of Jesus' love in our personal lives.

Not only each individual but the Church as a whole has the obligation to bear these fruits of love in the world. Pope Benedict XVI wrote in his first encyclical that the Church herself has a mission of love: "Love of neighbor, grounded in the love of God . . . is also a responsibility for the entire ecclesial community at every level: from the local community to the particular Church and to the Church universal in her entirety. As a community, the Church must practice love."[1] He went on to say that we can contribute to a better world only by personally doing good now, with full commitment and wherever we have the opportunity. Living the works of mercy accomplishes this goal.

2. To Build a "Civilization of Love and Truth"

As we have already seen, this is one of the themes that Pope John Paul II frequently emphasized, namely, that to be faithful followers of Jesus we need to build a civilization based on the Christian values of love and truth. When the Holy Spirit came at Pentecost, he created such a community among the very first disciples of Jesus gathered in Jerusalem for that great feast. Despite their ethnic, cultural, and language differences, the effect of the Spirit's coming was to restore a unity of peace and charity that had suffered greatly because of Original Sin and personal sin. Sin tends to separate while love tends to unite. In these critical times, we are well aware of the danger of violence, terrorism, and the whole culture of death, including the possible catastrophe of a nuclear war. Prayer, sacrifice, and reparation are essential to countering the negative effects of selfishness and sin in the world. But we must also reach out in a very concrete way to those who are in need. Practicing the works of mercy helps us to move out of a self-centeredness which emphasizes and focuses only on one's own personal needs and concerns, and directs us out toward the needs and concerns of others. It is through the daily living of these works of mercy and love that we will heal the ravages of war, of hatred, of violence, and ultimately of sinfulness. If we are to spread the King-

[1] Pope Benedict XVI, *God Is Love: Deus Caritas Est* (Libreria Editrice Vaticana: 2006; San Francisco: Ignatius Press, 2006), par. 20.

dom of God we must do the works of mercy that the Lord has taught us. Like the effect of yeast in a mound of dough, the values of the gospel will enter into and transform the culture and values of our society. The desired result will be a world where peace and charity will reign.

Pope John Paul II would also emphasize that peace requires the recognition and respect of the God-given dignity of each person. In other words, there can be no peace without justice. The works of mercy provide us with the opportunity to let all persons know they are children of our Heavenly Father as well as the brothers and sisters of Christ. What will emerge from this will be a community centered on and united in the love and peace of Christ himself. This is what prompted Saint Augustine to say that "in the end, there will be only one Christ loving himself." This means that the love Jesus shares with us and makes real in our hearts will be shared with one another, beginning here on earth and then for all eternity in Heaven.

3. To Work Out Our Salvation

In the Book of Deuteronomy, Moses set before the people the Lord's commandments. He then told the Israelites: "See, I have set before you this day life and good, death and evil. If you obey the commandments of the LORD your God which I command you this day, by loving the LORD your God, by walking in his ways, and by keeping his commandments and his statutes and his ordinances, then you shall live" (Deut 30:15–16). In a similar way Jesus tells us in his Gospel account of the final judgment that he has set before us: the choice of life and death in terms of whether we carry out the works of mercy or not.

The Lord tells us that at the Last Judgment we will

receive eternal reward or punishment depending on whether we have served him or neglected him in his neediest brothers and sisters. The Lord says he will separate those who have loved him by the practice of the works of mercy from those who have neglected him, like a shepherd separating sheep from goats. He will say to those who failed to love him:

> "Depart from me, you cursed, into the eternal fire prepared for the devil and his angels; for I was hungry and you gave me no food, I was thirsty and you gave me no drink, I was a stranger and you did not welcome me, naked and you did not clothe me, sick and in prison, and you did not visit me."
> (Mt 25:41-43)

We certainly do not want to be on that side because they "will go off to eternal punishment"!

Rather, let us strive to live the works of mercy that we may hear Jesus tell us: "I was hungry and you gave me food, I was thirsty and you gave me drink, I was a stranger and you welcomed me, I was naked and you clothed me, I was sick and you visited me, I was in prison and you came to me" (Mt 25:35-36). Pope John Paul II said that human history as we know it will end when Jesus says: "Truly I say to you, as you did it to one of the least of these my brethren, you did it to me" (Mt 25:40). If we do these things, we may hope to be among the righteous who will go to eternal life!

OH Gracious and Holy Father